POWER IN PSYCHOTHERAPEUTIC PRACTICE

POWER IN PSYCHOTHERAPEUTIC PRACTICE

David Heller, Ph.D.

HUMAN SCIENCES PRESS, INC.
72 FIFTH AVENUE
NEW YORK, N.Y. 10011

Library of Congress Cataloging in Publication Data

Heller, David.
    Power in psychotherapeutic practice.

    Bibliography: p.
    Includes index.
    1. Psychotherapist and patient. 2. Control (Psy-
chology) I. Title. [DNLM: 1. Authoritarianism.
2. Psychotherapy—methods. WM 420 H477p]
    RC480.8.H45   1985   616.89'14   84-10811
    ISBN 0-89885-228-5

In testament to the often power-laden
hours spent in search of myself

CONTENTS

ABOUT THE TITLES

11

The Reigns of Power ....President Abraham Lincoln, in *In Reply to the Missouri Committee of Seventy* (1864)

The Power is Thine ....*The New Testament*: Matthew 6:13

PREFACE

Power would seem a crucial as well as contemporary inroad into the nature of psychotherapy. In May of 1971, the Scientific Meeting of the American Academy of Psychoanalysis described the following scenario for psychotherapy in our era: "A patient often comes to us for help to enhance the quality of his life, or to alleviate the suffering which comes from a deficit of power or the tyrannical imposition of power over him. Power dynamics must be one of the basic concerns in psychotherapy" (*The Dynamics of Power*, 1972).

Nevertheless, the psychotherapy field largely overlooks or minimizes discussion of therapist power. This irony appears as true for clinical practice as well as for research. The neglect of discussion traverses the various comparative approaches to psychotherapy and the diverse therapies for individual populations, for children and adults alike. Consequently, the avoidance of power from open appraisal is a recurrent and pervasive theme —one which highlights the need for the present essay.

Therapist power demands consideration from a variety of perspectives and our discussion stands as an introductory response to this necessity. From the clinical world, we concentrate heavily on a psychoanalytic approach to psychotherapy both because of its great impact and because of my own familiarity with its various forms. A consequence is the emergence of many observations which are perhaps most suitably intended for individual psychoanalytic therapy for adults. Yet, we also extensively discuss the client-centered and behavior therapy perspectives, and to a lesser extent, gestalt, behavioral-cognitive, and eclectic contributions. When relevant and illustrative, contributions from general psychology appear and substantiate or qualify clinical discourses. Readings from the humanities and other social sciences appear throughout and help further to develop and enliven our conceptualization of power. Our purpose, then, is to capture this rather ubiquitous notion called "power" in its rich complexity and entertain its meaning for therapy.

I. THE PRACTICE OF POWER

THE PRACTICE OF POWER

The most striking oversight in the field of psychotherapy has been the great neglect of power—an omission from open consideration in professional journals, clinical forums, training, supervision, and in psychotherapy sessions themselves. Several prominent spokespersons in the behavioral sciences have been emphatic concerning the seriousness of this omission. The more philosophical Rollo May sees the problem on a societal level: "I find that power is a subject we Americans don't like to discuss. We sweep it under the carpet, hide and repress it as we used to repress the discussion of death" (1979). David McClelland sees the difficulty as intrinsic to the field of psychotherapy: "By appearing to be without much power psychotherapy avoids outward accusations about power" (1973). Perhaps bringing together these perspectives, sociologist David Kipnis writes in his book *The Powerholder*: "Most people see power as representing the irrational, neurotic and perverted aspects of man's nature" (1974). However intractable the reasons for neglect may seem, it is unmistakably time for the avoidance of power to cease.

Other than such insightful general observations, professionals and patrons of psychotherapy have little scholarly literature and few personal accounts to rely upon concerning the role of power. Power seems to be one of those quiescent contributions to psychotherapy that most practitioners are aware of but few speak about. While a sleeping giant in therapies of any duration, power may be as much as part of the landscape of healing as empathy or understanding, more than an artifact of a particular approach or technique. Thus, my purpose is to explore and demystify the power of the psychotherapist, and in so doing, further a more informed understanding of the process of change.

As you read on, it is possible to find support for a view of power as harmful or even sinful in psychotherapy; it is equally possible to find evidence which favors a therapeutic view of power or a qualified stance which may seem more tenable. Yet I believe it is impossible to dismiss the clearly fundamental role power plays in psychotherapy. Even given the myriad appearances power may have, it stands out as a universal in a discipline that is renowned, if not infamous, for its diversity.

THE CONCERNS OF CLIENT AND THERAPIST

When you consider what most people fear about psychotherapy before they actually participate in the process, the question of power is likely at the heart of their apprehensions. Any person who enters therapy, however tentatively, is no foreigner to the feeling of powerlessness in the face of life circumstances. It seems that therapy-related expectations will follow naturally from perceived imbalance in everyday relationships. In the darkest of psychotherapy scenarios, a client may nightmarishly fantasize that the therapist will employ nefarious means to try to change him or her. Rarely does a client arrive in the practitioner's office without some reservation, though the extent of concern varies greatly.

From evaluation sessions that I have conducted, certain highlights seem representative. An older female client on the occasion of our initial meeting commented: "You, being so young, probably think that people change really easily. . . . But once you reach and pass middle age like me, well. . . . No one has a right to expect you to change so much. . . ." A thirty-year-old man, considering a possible divorce, was less explicit about his wariness, at least at first: "No, I don't have any questions . . . I feel like this will be okay . . . I don't know if I want a divorce, but I would like to find out about myself . . . I need to talk things out . . . [pause] Oh, by the way, you don't use any of that unconscious stuff, do you?" While perhaps more colorful in their respective deliveries than other clients, these individuals well captured the typical and commonplace fears concerning the application of therapist power.

Aside from the client's apprehensions, therapists too come to the therapeutic encounter with their own fears. One of the most prevalent unspoken preoccupations concerns power. What if, in an aggravated moment or unwittingly, the therapist imposes the shadow of his or her own world-view on the client? Therapists in and out of supervision and consultation quietly shudder at the thought of therapist coercion—so much so that often little is actually processed and discussed. Owing to early historical cautions in regard to therapeutic overinvolvement, pervasive in such disparate traditions as the psychoanalytic and client-centered schools, therapists tend to dread consideration of power and substantial personal investment as well. As a professional coterie, they seem to fear that their own preferences will adversely and inappropriately enter into their practice of psychotherapy. A widespread concern among individual therapists of most orientations, the fear of power is a troublesome issue for the profession as a whole. Such an atmosphere of caution and concern, along with the a priori doubts of clients concerning power, beckons for a careful consideration of therapist power and its neglect.

THE CHAPTERS ON THERAPIST POWER

To begin to describe and understand the presence of power in psychotherapy, we must first try to clarify what we mean by the word "power." Yet power is too meaningful and too comprehensive a notion to define very easily and succinctly, particularly given its sometimes diverse and sometimes antithetical meanings. Thus, the definitional concerns of power represent the starting point for the chapters that follow. In addition to describing power, we need to differentiate power from other related phenomena that may be confused with power or accompany it in the clinical setting. Aggression, mastery, and nurturance are examples of such affective phenomena. Also, as power seems to consist of several dimensions of experience it becomes imperative to offer a basic understanding of the differences among feelings, thoughts, and acts of power.

At the outset, we also will examine what theorists and philosophers have contributed concerning the notion of power. From Emerson to Erikson, scholars have struggled with the essence of power in the individual and the nature of power in society. Indeed, power seems everpresent in human affairs and prominent in the minds of those who speculate and write about human affairs. While the contributions of psychologists are of foremost interest for this inquiry, the philosophical roots of our conceptions are also included to provide a sense of the breadth of influences.

A more directed attention to clinical psychological writing begins with the question of why power has been so generally denied and avoided. The question is disturbing and in many ways surprising. After all else has been considered, psychotherapy is essentially an arena for the seemingly powerless to seek assistance in psychological predicaments. Hence, it presents a forum in which one person calls on another for direction in finding the power to change; psychotherapy would seem a fertile ground for the unfolding and mutual discussion of power dynamics. However, this is not always the case.

While some psychotherapy approaches may attend to the power contributions of the client, few are consistently sensitive to the realistic power contributions made by the therapist. Moreover, the psychotherapy literature also reflects this insensitivity by its neglect of therapist power issues. We attempt to address the neglect in light of the more general hesitance concerning therapists' feelings. It seems that the field's relationship to power belongs in the broader context of its relationship to the therapeutic reactions of the practitioner.

A thorough examination of psychotherapy necessitates substantial consideration of sources of power, those origins of power behind the scene in the clinical setting. Perhaps locating all of the sources of power at a given moment in therapy is impossible. Indicating some of the most common sources is not only possible, however, but most educational and useful.

The more global sources of power in psychotherapy are cultural. Cultural expectations concerning the role of therapist, the modern-day practitioner of ritual healing, provide some of the bases for therapist power (Bromberg, 1962). As a culture, we seem to bestow upon therapists many special powers and anticipate that they will implement these powers as part of their societally-defined role.

A second contributing area for sources of power is the realm of therapeutic technique. Theories of technique, those competing perspectives within the institution of psychotherapy, present a foundation for therapist power no less influential than cultural ambience. In particular, training ethos, therapist role definition, and intervention procedures all work together to create a climate for therapeutic power. Considering the formidable variety of available treatment approaches, economy demands that we concentrate on the best known of these perspectives: the psychoanalytic, the client-centered, and the behavioral approaches.

As a third source of therapist power, individual personality acts as the ultimate filter through which cultural and institutional powers are communicated (Burton, 1975). Unequivocally, the personal qualities of the therapist as well as those of the client tend to contribute greatly to the power and outcome of what develops between them. In this discussion, we are interested not only in personality concerns like the need for power but also demographic issues like sex and age, which are probable factors contributing to the individual's experience of power. As with the inquiry in its entirety, we concentrate on the neglected topic of the therapist's personal contributions in our chapters on sources of power. Concerning this emphasis, Jerome Frank poses an intriguing thought for his readers to entertain in *Persuasion and Healing*: "Finally, the possibility must be recognized that some of the most powerful healing components in psycho-therapy may lie in the qualities of the therapist—such as, per-haps, innate healing power" (1973).

Closely related to these several sources of power are the many forms of power manifestations. Such manifestations of power reflect its actual pragmatic effects and appearances in the therapy setting. Since manifestations are perhaps limitless in scope and variety, we entertain the most likely forms. Each ther-apist and client dyad may demonstrate its own unique man-ner of interaction, and even such hypothetical patterns of power communication are subject to incessant variations depending on life and therapy-related circumstances. Some therapy pairs, for example, will be comfortably verbal with each other until devel-oping tensions direct the expression of power toward more non-verbal or indirect expressions. Other participants, depending upon treatment approach and the individual personalities, may be principally verbal in communication. Thus the possible ways a therapist may experience reactions of power are very numer-ous and may well harbor pronounced impact on the therapeutic process.

Given this vast array of possibilities, the most informative discussion of power manifestations at present would be a cata-logue of types of power expression. In attempting this overview, the discussion of manifestations will begin with the structural as-pects of the clinical setting. By structural contributions, we refer to those elements of the psychotherapy situation that portray personal qualities of the therapist or qualities of the therapeutic technique. For example, office decor and treatment atmosphere are two such structural aspects of psychotherapy.

Following along with these structural considerations, verbal manifestations of power are part and parcel of perhaps all con-ventional psychotherapies (Lennard & Bernstein, 1960). In ad-dition to the most overt expressions of power, we will want to consider the sometimes overlooked place of paralinguistic or verbal-related qualities of speech. Language structure, for in-stance, is an area especially in need of greater study in psycho-therapy investigations. Language structure refers to the choice and order of therapist words made in the service of therapeutic interventions or other therapy-related dialogue.

It is currently becoming quite clear that nonverbal cues must assume their proper position alongside verbal concerns in the therapy process. Nonverbal manifestations are basic ingredients in therapy and are likely to represent a major contribution to therapeutic power. On the importance of nonverbal cues, social psychologist Sharon Brehm concludes an informed outsider's view of clinical practice with the following thought: "In virtually every form of psychotherapy, it seems there are occasions when the therapist attempts to influence the client through nonverbal (and verbal) persuasion" (1976). Discussion of a selection of nonverbal channels, including postures and facial cues, closes our compendium of power manifestations.

In light of its many sources and manifestations, the uses and abuses of power in psychotherapeutic practice emerge for theoretical and practical review. The fears and concerns of therapist and client alike suggest that power can indeed be therapeutic as well as countertherapeutic. In the realm of psychotherapy, power may represent, at one extreme, the mainstay in the curative physician's bag of the therapist. At the other extreme, power may become a hazardous weapon that misfires and psychologically injures the client. Thus, the study of power is likely to have numerous implications for the unfolding clinical process and for the practice of psychotherapy as a discipline. These implications are treated with regard to each of several areas: the field as a whole; the place of technique in psychotherapy; and the nature of the therapeutic relationship.

Discussion of the implications of power serves as a necessary concluding point for this introductory venture into the world of power in psychotherapy. While our consideration of power in psychotherapeutic practice draws to a close with this final chapter, in its entirety this compendium represents only a beginning point for continual introspection—a basis for self-examination, whether the reader is a therapist, a client, or both.

Chapter 1

CONCEPTIONS OF POWER
The Will to Power

The concept of power poses an exceedingly complex definitional problem. Concerning its precise meaning, social scientist
Robert Bierstedt observes: "In the entire lexicon of sociological
concepts, none is more troublesome than the concept of power.
We may say about it in general only what St. Augustine said
about time, that we all know perfectly well what it is—until
someone asks us" (1950).

Psychology alone reveals a plethora of descriptions, each of
which seems to categorize power along various behavioral or
motivational dimensions (e.g., French and Raven [1959] postulate five bases for power). There is a constant struggle in the literature between a view of power as a singular, coherent phenomenon and a view of power as multidimensional (Rowan,
1976). Undoubtedly, an understanding of power is further com-
plicated by the role of power in both humanitarian and malevo-
lent acts. The literature concerning power, in articulating
diverse conceptions of power, provides a useful forum for discussion although definitive conclusions are rarely presented. We
now review some of the key contributions in search of a shared
definitional focus for the notion of power.

THE SCHOLARLY LITERATURE

Philosophical Origins

The modern conception of a benign power has its roots in the field of philosophy and in Nietzsche's notion of "will to power." While he maintains that man's strivings represent a compensation for the death of God, Nietzsche emphasizes man's capacity for self-assertion and self-transcendence. He views the "will to power" as a quality inherent in the very substance of man, a characteristic which forges opportunity for man and foreshadows what will become of him. This concern with man's future also indicates a preoccupation with man's relationship with man. Thus, in Nietzsche's conceptualization, power is thought to be a shared and highly socialized characteristic. Power does not refer to a dominance over other men: Nietzsche is careful to rule this out (Tillich, 1954).

The idea of power over others, of controlling and dictating the course of events for others, invariably brings up the name of Machiavelli, author of *Discourses* and *The Prince* (1640). These crowning works of the famous political theorist stand as caricatures of the more banal applications of power. Through his view of man, Machiavelli depicts man as a largely fearful but reactively ambitious creature. Above all, man is apprehensive about other men and is therefore anxious to dominate them. Even when there is no necessity to assert power, Machiavelli contends, power will be exercised as a matter of habit or instinct. While proposing the need for some men to rule over others for the good of civilization, Machiavelli steadfastly argues that the need for power can never be satisfied—man is inevitably too fearful of others to maintain a sense of security (Sampson, 1965).

Psychological Origins

A series of psychological descriptions of power suggest opposing faces of power and further elaborate the concept. A forerunner in psychology concerning power was Alfred Adler, who maintained early on that the striving for power resulted from the need to compensate for perceived inferiority (Adler, 1927).

Adler asserts that power is an organizing principle of life which is essential for personal and group esteem. He speaks to the interpersonal aspects of power while addressing its clinical implications. In his seminal contribution *Superiority and Social Interest*, Adler concludes: "Deviations and neuroses are forms of expression for such [power] striving directed against fellowmanship" (1927). The Adlerian conception of power thus focuses on a power that arises out of powerlessness, but does not recognize a more spontaneous and self-asserted position of impact.

Among other prominent voices, Harry Stack Sullivan is representative of those psychologists who called for an alternative view of human power. Sullivan is adamant about the interpersonal nature of power. He distinguishes between social circumstances in which power arises out of fear, a type of power close to the Adlerian concept, and circumstances which create power out of a sense of security and strength. In *The Interpersonal Theory of Psychiatry*, Sullivan argues that some power feelings of the second order represent a motive force in the service of cultural and personal accomplishment (Sullivan, 1953). By highlighting man's power to work in conjunction with man, Sullivan and other writers began to challenge a thoroughly negative conception of power and began to suggest the adaptive uses of power.

During the past 2 decades, other theorists and researchers have traced the nature of power and have emphasized a multidimensional conception of power. Within social psychology, conceptual distinctions tend to be based on sources of power or based on the grounds by which power is attained. Each author or set of authors seems to place their own particular stamp on a more basic distinction concerning power.

For example, Wilkins and DeCharms (1962) postulate "internal" and "external" bases of power. Internal power refers to "power accruing to the individual qua individual" (1962). A person equipped with internal power possesses a fundamental and lasting sense of impact. The power is inherent. Such individuals do not seek power for themselves alone but naturally apply power for a higher goal. In contrast, external power is "power accruing to the individual in accordance with the position the individual holds and his possession of societally valued objects or experiences" (1962).

With particular emphasis, Wilkins and DeCharms maintain and empirically demonstrate a positive relationship between authoritarianism and external power (represented by position or status). The authors suggest that the relationship is strongest in the absence of substantial internal power. If we apply this finding to the clinical setting, which is yet to be tested, we might anticipate finding a similar relationship between therapists' consciousness of their therapist status and the source of their power, whether internal or external.

An equally well-known investigation concerning the nature of power is the contribution of French and Raven (1959). The central purpose of this paper is the delineation of five bases of power. "Referent power" is power based on an individual's desire to emulate another person because of perceived inner qualities. Referent power is considered to be highly socialized since it is freely chosen and shared. Meanwhile, "coercive power" is power attributed to another person because an individual is manipulated into doing so. Coercive power represents an apparent misuse of power since volition is unnecessary for its emergence. With the enactment of this form of power, the recipient's welfare is not taken into account. The French and Raven scheme suggests a crucial point concerning typologies of power and concerning the nature of power: without an understanding of the inner sources of power for the individual, overt behavioral manifestations of power are insufficient to determine the usefulness or harmfulness of a given application of power.

From the psychology of personality and motivation, the contributions of McClelland (1973) and Winter (1973) provide a dual conceptualization of power motivation. These authors, most instrumental in our appreciation of the achievement motive as well, postulate and validate two types of power motive. The first, a "leadership motive," reflects a hope for power and a desire to utilize power for the advancement of others. Closely allied with achievement or feelings of competency, leadership power permits others to possess power in their own right. The exercise of leadership power means that an individual treats others like "origins" of their own actions rather than "pawns" of his or her actions. The leadership motive implies a concern about the uses of power and the misuses, as if the powerholder protects all concerned against abusive expressions of power (Mc-Clelland, 1973).

The concept of "dominance power" is largely based on an individual's fear of extrinsic or foreign power (McClelland, 1973). Dominance power is characterized by the pursuit of victory over active adversaries and the delegation of others to threatening situations. The actor in dominance power defensively perceives the world as a zero-sum game and stresses the incessant competitiveness of the world. Other people are treated as pawns during the exercise of dominance power. There is a preoccupation with issues of coercion and submission and a balance of power cannot be tolerated. According to McClelland (1973), the individual sometimes balances on a "knife-edge" between socialized or dominance power. What this observation suggests is that the two kinds of power must be highly related and in practice difficult to discern from one another. Both McClelland and Winter are emphatic about this point. As we shall later elaborate, the observation also seems to hold true for the individual psychotherapist in the clinical setting.

In addition to Alfred Adler and Harry Stack Sullivan, a few modern clinical psychologists have addressed the nature of power and have attested to its profound clinical importance. Schimel (1972), Salzman (1972), and May (1972) have all independently described clinical experiences which illustrate the theoretical distinction proposed by researchers in other areas of psychology and by their clinical forebears.

These contemporary practitioners all describe, on one hand, a type of power that is consonant with healthy personality development and high self-esteem. The individual who demonstrates such power carries great weight in interpersonal affairs and can endure ambivalence and uncertainty. On the other hand, the authors describe a type of power that is more coercive. Salzman (1972) refers to this form of power as "power over others." In such a case, power is manipulated either in fact or with intent. Power over others is associated with a weak personality, low self-esteem and an impaired capacity for intimate relations. Great apprehension and anxiety accompany this form of power, according to the clinicians, and there emerges a continual conflict within the self over power (Schimel, 1972).

Implicitly in their writings, these clinical authors consistently underscore that both forms of power occur spontaneously in the clinical setting and are essential to what psychotherapy should be concerned with. In summarizing their observations, as well as the sometimes antithetical nature of power, Salzman (1972) explains:

> Feelings of power may be essential in overcoming attitudes of helplessness, powerlessness, and the total dependency of the infant or child. Only through the development of one's ability or feeling of power in these earlier years can we have sufficient faith in our capacity to deal with later situations . . . [but] power, like other human capacities, can become a participant in compulsive [neurotic] processes. When it does, it has greater potential for good or for evil, since compulsivity involves passionate intensity and exclusive preoccupation as well as rigidity, inflexibility and a devotion to the process rather than the person. (p. 162)

A Composite Definition

The scholarly literature concerning power presents several definitional pathways and yields important areas for common conceptual ground. Bringing together some of these diverse theoretical contributions suggests a working definition of power. This definition will describe power in the broadest sense and will emphasize the inclusion of even apparently paradoxical power phenomena. At the same time, we will try to adhere to the features that make power a unique human experience. Power becomes a particularly useful concept when it encompasses a wide range of experiences and yet is recognizable from related phenomena such as aggression. Thus, in light of the scholarly literature and with special sensitivity to its relevance for psychotherapy, the concept of power during our discussion will refer to the following general condition:

> A quality of possessing intentional and meaningful impact in relation to the self, others, and the environment.

What now seems most helpful is to examine each aspect of the definition.

"Impact" is a central notion for the concept. An impact is an outcome, effect, or result; it is the consequence of the individual will of the agent of power. Since impacts may occur in several possible forms, we may say that impacts appear: during behavioral activity; with the inhibition of behavioral activity; during cognitive information processing; with the inhibition of cognitive processing; and along with emotional tension or the release of emotional tension. An example of an act in the inhibitory realms would be refraining from an incisive comment during a conversation or the defensive repression of a past event. One of the most subtle ways in which a therapist may have impact is by precluding from discussion attributions that the client makes about him- or herself and an unhappy personal state.

Of equal importance to the definition, "intentionality" indicates a causal and real linkage between this eventual impact and the power actor's inner state. The actor must be able to govern or mediate this relationship for power to be present. The notion of the willfulness of the actor is fundamental to power—a necessary though not a sufficient condition in itself. Even impacts of great magnitude and change, such as those that might accompany a religious conversion experience, would not be demonstrations of power unless the actor intends change to occur.

According to Rollo May (1969), the intentionality inherent in power may be understood as a response to determinism though deterministic forces must simultaneously be taken into account. Intentionality in the clinical setting is perhaps best illustrated by the therapist's steady drive to facilitate personality change in the client.

The "meaningfulness" of an impact suggests that the impact must indeed have subjective significance for the participants. In other words, the outcome must not be trivial but must harbor perceived importance for those it affects.[1] Concerns about work and family life tend to trigger high emotional involvement, and thus the potential for meaningful impact in conjunction with such circumstances is substantial. In general, it is not necessary for the object of power explicitly to agree with the actor with regard to the meaningfulness of an outcome, though consensus ordinarily increases the actor's felt sense of power.

In psychotherapy sessions, the meaningfulness of a given issue will vary greatly depending upon the participants and the nature of their task. Major life decisions which are mutually discussed, such as choosing to have a child, asking for a divorce, or making a major career change, might be considered universally meaningful. The psychotherapist who plays an involved role in such decisions will ordinarily accumulate great power.

As the first target of power, the "self" refers to the powerholder, the actor, or the agent of power. In some cases, outcomes of concern are the intrapersonal experiences of the powerholder; in such a circumstance the self is the object of power. When the self is the object or target of power socialization, as when an individual tries to "gain control over" him- or herself, then that individual is both agent and recipient. In psychotherapy, the self may refer to either the person of the therapist or the person of the client. In conventional psychotherapy-related publications, much attention has been paid to the self of the client (e.g., the client-centered notion of an "ideal self"), but the therapist is not commonly considered in such an objective fashion.

Along with the self, "others" are the most common targets of power. Others are so important for power because of power's interpersonal nature: power is a phenomenon which has intentionality toward an external object and this object is frequently another person. In such a case, an impact on the other person may also have impact for the power agent, though in psychotherapy this is not always true. Sometimes therapists may have impact on their clients without having any pronounced socialization effect on themselves. Typical others in psychotherapy include a vast panorama of characters, including parents, siblings, spouses, children, job cohorts, friends, and, of course, therapists and clients.

Lastly, the "environment" as a target of power refers to outcomes in the nonhuman world. An actor engaged in power may experience impact in relation to animals, inanimate objects, the natural environment, and a host of miscellaneous objects (e.g., limits of time and space, laws of the sensory or kinesthetic realms). Environmental targets of power are included so that the definition of power may cover the full scope of power experiences. Phobias, such as a fear of flying or a fear of heights, are among the most frequently appearing conditions in psychotherapy which reflect a lack of power over environmental circumstances, as well as an internal power struggle.

THE DIMENSIONS OF POWER

Power appears in the various dimensions of an individual's experience—affective, motivational, cognitive, and behavioral. Here, we start with the affective realm since feelings often seem to occur first[2] within the individual and we then move toward actual power behavior.

Feelings of power comprise an individual's current or retrieved sensory experience of harboring impact. Colloquially, this type of phenomenon in psychotherapy is sometimes referred to as a "gut reaction," a "sense," or an "impression." Even outside of the therapy context, power feelings ordinarily coexist with feelings of satisfaction derived from the shaping of outcomes or averting the loss of potential impact (Christie & Geis, 1971). Among their many properties, power feelings initiate an ongoing motivational state: this motive state stirs an individual toward the exercise of the feeling (Izard & Tompkins, 1965). Such feelings may occur without much prior thought about power or about the objects of power, but most often feelings develop in conjunction with such thoughts (Zajonc, 1980). A feeling of power may also be transient or it may be tracelike, sometimes persisting long after its initial appearance. For instance, a therapist's initial power over an influential intervention may last long after the actual impact has subsided, as may the sense of satisfaction.

Feelings of power are intimately related to power motivation. Power motives may be understood as "generalized dispositions or tendencies toward having impact and may involve some prediction concerning impact" (Winter, 1973). Feelings seem to activate power motives in the individual. While feelings seem to reflect a current or recollected experience, motives appear to be the agents of feeling that anticipate impact and seek out targets for the discharge of feeling. Like swift-footed Mercury, the

Greek messenger god, motives often carry with them traces of the feeling experience and relay these traces through other dimensions of experience.

Individuals seem to differ markedly in their respective drives toward power, depending upon the effects of early parental socialization (Winter, 1973). We might also anticipate that therapists too will show clear differences in motivation, although their shared attraction to the therapy process and profession may tend to minimize such differences.

The cognitive dimension of power regulates power communications and power-related information. As several now famous studies have shown, cognitions may occur independently of feelings or actions (e.g., see Schacter and Singer, 1965). Within the cognitive realm, data about the capacity for impact may be encoded in mental compartments or schemas, organized structures which portray and store knowledge. Commonly, schemas include conceptual structures about the self and about others in relation to power.

It is important to note that these schemas are profoundly shaped and colored by past learning and experience (Markus, 1981). For therapists, then, the schemas would be influenced by theoretical orientation and professional training and socialization. Thus, a psychoanalytically-trained therapist might associate his sense of power to the discovery of oedipal complexes. Schematically pairing this dynamic construct with a sense of power, he might be further inclined to look for oedipal imagery in his clients' presentations, which would enhance his experience of power.

In contrast to thoughts of power, behavioral power is the action of power itself rather than the internal awareness of its presence. While it may sometimes be subtly expressed, behavioral power is more graphically embodied by the monarch's assenting nod or the symphony conductor's arm gesture. Regular patterns of behavior like walking demeanor or seating manner are typically associated with feelings of power, though an individual may express power without being consciously aware of doing so. An individual may also be cognizant of power, experience it affectively, but choose not to act upon these inner phenomena. The kinship between behavior and feeling is most

apparent in the various behavior therapies. In counterconditioning, behavior modification or other related practices, a directed change in behavior also seems to induce a change in the
client's affective state as well (Lazarus, 1971).

THE RELATIONSHIP BETWEEN POWER AND OTHER CONCEPTS

In social interaction and in clinical discourse, power
rarely seems to emerge in isolation but more often arises along
with the development of other phenomena. These other phenomena may occur naturally with power and share common
characteristics, yet they are difficult to discriminate from power.
For our purposes, understanding these related phenomena provides yet an additional way of describing power. The concepts of
"aggression," "nurturance," and "mastery" are of particular interest because of their self-assertive or self-ascendant qualities.

Aggression is most simply thought of as the intention of
harm or injury to others in order to banish a source of fear
(Baron, 1977). Like power, aggressive feelings contain an element of intention: self-agency of an actor is essential as the actor
desires to thrust or direct him- or herself forward. Both power
and aggression are ordinarily aimed at protecting the rights and
dominion of the self, though in power these territories need not
be considered in jeopardy by the actor. In the course of pursu-
ing goals, power and aggression frequently inspirit some form
of ecstasy—e.g., the sense of heightened excitement associated
with wartime or the sense of exultation linked to more socialized
encounters like sports events.

Rollo May (1972) describes such a sense of manic triumph
while clarifying the distinction between power and aggression.
To achieve this theoretical clarification, psychotherapist May
relies on the example of Herman Melville's well-known novel,
Billy Budd. The essence of May's illustration follows: following
the death of Billy Budd, the British, his comrades, inexplicably
cheer the sight of the approaching French warships. According
to May, the British are filled with latent hostility and are eager
for release. Thus, they experience euphoria over the opportunity to vent aggression and exert themselves once again. While

the aggression is more apparent, there also emerges a struggle with power out of the depths of powerlessness; thus, both power and aggression are at work and are related to this ineffable sense of excitement (May, 1972).

Despite their interface, power and aggression are not synonymous. While power principally implies a sense of impact, aggression suggests a desire to abolish or vanquish a perceived threat. While power intends an ongoing relationship with its object, aggression typically does not seek such an association with its target. Thus, power relationships, like those between employees and management, require the continued participation of both sides. Aggression phenomena do not: employers fire their workers and consequently terminate any further involvement.

Power also seems to develop out of an already existing sense of power; aggression, on the other hand, seems to surface chiefly out of the fear of threat or the potential loss of power (Veroff & Veroff, 1972). Hence, an aggressive individual tries to accomplish a restructuring of power. Aggression erupts when that individual or a group of individuals believes that change cannot happen through the affirmation of power alone. For example, a therapist may resort to the insidious aggression of a sarcastic comment when more power-oriented attempts at clarification have been frustrated by the client.

Nurturance also commonly arises or develops in psychotherapy, but unlike aggression, is often associated with beneficent applications of power. A definition of nurturance would invariably focus upon the desire to make others feel comfortable, accepted, and approved (Rollins & Thomas, 1975). Like the experience of power, nurturance involves in significant fashion the object of nurturance or its recipient. Nurturance fosters a new and more satisfied state in the object; power seeks a new state of power or a condition of powerlessness in its target. Of particular interest for psychotherapy is the tendency for power to accompany nurturance in actual interaction. A bearer of emotional sustenance tends to have great impact on those who need comfort or approval (McClelland, 1973).

However, nurturance differs from power in its de-emphasis on the actor and the nature of the intention. The nurturant person does not pursue self-enhancement as a primary incentive in itself, and thus is less self-focused than the powerholder. The nurturant person concentrates on the recipient while the powerful person concentrates on the relationship between actor and target.

It should also be noted that nurturance can appear without the concomitant presence of power. For example, work with autistic children requires the provision of considerable giving without any recognition of this impact by the child or any evidence of impact. Most often, however, power and nurturance commonly arise together in psychotherapy. This kinship is particularly visible in supportive therapies which produce therapists who are viewed as powerfully helping and giving.[3]

Mastery is a third phenomenon that tends to be related to power in the clinical situation. Like power and aggression, mastery is a self-assertive motive. It refers to an individual's sense of coping effectively and independently with an environmental task (White, 1979). Mastery requires a certain willfulness on the part of the actor. Just as the powerful actor tries to have impact, the achieving individual strives to perform the designated task with proficiency.

With both power and mastery, the actor's consciousness of the outcome is required for a true inner experiencing of the phenomenon. When a small boy in child therapy builds a castle, for example, he develops feelings of mastery only if he attributes the fourteenth-century replica to his own creativity. He won't experience mastery if he sees the outcome as due to the efforts of the therapist or due to a serendipitous arrangement of building toys. Mastery, like power, increases self-esteem as it seeks to enhance self-perception through personal accomplishment.

Nevertheless, mastery does not focus upon other people in the way that power does. Mastery implies only a relationship to a task per se while power takes into account the social world as well. The quest for mastery leads to concern over abstract criteria or standards of excellence, achievement tasks to be entertained and accomplished by one's own efforts (Veroff, 1980). On the other hand, the pursuit of power coincides with a concern about self-standards or the standards of other significant figures.

While mastery may occur in the presence of others, it requires no sense of empathy with other achievers. While power and mastery resemble each other in their twin emphases on self-directedness and drive toward self-esteem, their difference can be summarized by power's interpersonal orientation relative to the more intrapersonal orientation of mastery.

Clinical approaches will differ considerably with regard to the comparative importance each places on mastery and power. Problem-solving and task-oriented techniques like "systematic desensitization" predominantly try to teach a mastery over established goals. The more insight-oriented techniques appeal to the power of the therapeutic relationship or to the power of self-examination. In this latter brand of psychotherapies, the practitioner tends to experience mastery in relation to understanding the therapeutic process or in relation to diagnostic discriminating, but power is more often experienced through the therapist's more direct impact on the client.

SUMMARY NOTES ON CONCEPTIONS OF POWER

A cursory sample of scholarly literature and analysis provides a working definition of power and a basis for a common understanding. Although such efforts at a theoretical foundation provide some shared language concerning power, they can only closely approximate the nature of power in psychotherapy. The psychotherapeutic situation presents a unique context for all interpersonal phenomena like power. As we embark on an exploration of these special circumstances in the next chapter, several crucial points should be remembered concerning our theoretical observations of power.

> (1) Power is not in itself a desire to conquer or care for others, though it may well accompany such aggressive or nurturant intentions. Power does not only infer an individual's resourcefulness against the environment but it also conveys the person's stance in social interaction. Above all, and this point is critical to its definition, power is not a feeling passively happened upon. On the contrary, power is a willful

and self-chosen experience which arises out of the desire to harbor impact upon life.

(2) The psychology literature in particular stresses the "intentionality" of power, i.e., that power is guided by the direction set forth by the powerholder. In psychotherapy, it becomes essential to consider the unconscious as well as the conscious intentions of the actor (the therapist).

(3) Much of the general literature points to the paradoxical nature of power, a feeling and an experience capable of fostering coercive acts as well as prosocial efforts. As we shall see, this possible duality has profound implications for a profession like psychotherapy, which asks of its individual practitioners nothing less than distinguishing between the use or abuse of power at any given moment.

Chapter 2

CONCEPTIONS OF THERAPIST REACTIONS
The Denial of Power

Power within the arena of psychotherapy is power within a most particular and specialized context. More than an abstract notion, power in therapy refers to those feelings of power experienced by a therapist (or by a client) as a result of therapeutic involvement. Such power naturally develops within the larger purview of a psychotherapist's emotional reactions and thus belongs along with the growing literature concerning such therapist contributions.

This literature of therapist reactions indicates few authors who view clinical observation as entirely free of a client's influence. Most clinicians seem to agree that the effects of the client do matter but they tend to differ on the degree to which therapist-client interaction is emphasized. Nearly all of the literature is inspired by a psychoanalytically-based view of personality. Under the common banner of "countertransference," which we will use here interchangeably with therapist reactions, a number of contributors have struggled earnestly with the topic of therapist feelings. Freud sometimes called this domain "the therapist's own individuality" (Freud, 1912).[1]

The countertransference literature reflects a reasonably

clear process of transformation: the focus shifts gradually from the therapist's pathological reactions (the classical view) to those responses that are induced by the client (the objective view), and then, to the totality of responses experienced by the therapist (the totalistic view). The literature continually articulates these several perspectives and each offers a certain important if limited insight into the nature of power. Following a discussion of the avoidance of therapists' feelings, these several trends are summarized and their relevance to power is noted.

THE DENIAL OF THERAPIST POWER REACTIONS

The pervasiveness of therapist reactions and its relationship to patient experience is well documented by a few contributors in the literature.[2] Within every moment of silence or within every interaction, there exists the potential for a therapist reaction, or so clinicians seem to suggest (Langs, 1976). Some even further assert that these reactions present a prerequisite for therapy; therapists may indeed respond to every event in the psychotherapeutic situation (Racker, 1957; Spitz, 1955; Berman, 1947). The central presence of such reactions would be far from surprising given the significance of external reactions in everyday discourse (Sandler, 1970; Bernstein & Burris, 1967). Moreover, clinicians seem to maintain, the clinical handling of therapist feelings may determine successful outcome in psychotherapy (Alger, 1966).

Despite their widespread presence, therapist reactions are still often denied or evaded by the majority of writers and perhaps by the majority of practitioners as well. Set aside from consideration, the therapist's contribution thus comprises an unspoken and neglected part of the healing process.

The historical scenario of psychoanalysis reveals a certain retreat from close examination, according to Benedek (1953), while it appears that the same could be said of the younger therapeutic approaches. For example, the client-centered view makes frequent reference to therapist feelings but evidences little in-depth attention to this area in its literature. Even during the 1950s, when therapist reactions attracted some new-found interest, less than 5 percent of all the articles in psychotherapy journals addressed the topic (Bernstein, 1958). While summarizing this oversight in his insightful work *The Bipersonal Field*, Robert Langs critically comments: ". . . there has been a tendency toward an appropriate imbalance in certain aspects of the therapist's assessment of the patient's communications as compared to his own" (1976).

The historical context of psychotherapy provides an initial explanation for its denial and neglect. The roots of psychotherapy and the philosophy of psychotherapy can be located in the field of medicine, which prioritizes scientific objectivity over personal subjectivity in response to the treatment of physical maladies. Under the rubric of the medical model, many therapists regard psychological difficulties as disorders which necessitate rational and technical intervention. A common approach requires the use of rational understanding to help resolve psychological distress, however irrational the origins of conflict may be. The age-old simile is still influential: like the surgeon who must isolate personal feelings from the task to be performed, the therapist must rely upon careful observation and intellectual acumen alone. As with the medical counterpart, the therapist must refrain from expression of private feelings.

The development of traditional psychoanalysis, with its analytic "mirror" and "neutral" persona emerging as corollaries to the physician's antiseptic stance, leaves little room for the role of therapist feelings. On the whole, psychoanalysis scorns these feelings as *verboten*[3] and criticizes their inappropriate emergence in psychoanalysis. According to the medical model perspective and its common application in psychoanalysis, such a policy on therapist reactions allows the therapist to maintain the cognitive bearing necessary to steer the course of the patient's pathology. A popular criticism of this view, however, suggests that some therapists may use the approach to circumnavigate their own personal anxieties, anxieties which are related to a release of cognitive control. Moreover, critics sometimes argue, if psychotherapy is portrayed as solely a technical process, the person of the therapist will be lost at sea. Certainly, it seems that few authors in the early years of psychotherapy were prepared to rescue the person of the therapist.

A second compelling reason for denial is the stereotypically negative connotation attached to therapist reactions. For some individual approaches, such as the behavioral techniques and the cognitive techniques, affects are not even considered a central area of concern for the client (Prochaska, 1979). In other comparative approaches, such as the psychoanalytically-oriented strategies, therapist feelings are treated as regretful intrusions into the flow of spontaneous client expressions. Thus, in these latter approaches, therapist affects are considered interferences which inadvertently arise during a session and unfortunately present a nemesis against even the best of therapeutic intentions.

With such pronounced emphasis on either the irrelevance or the obstructiveness of therapist reactions in the field, many practitioners seem to grow reticent concerning the open discussion of their reactions. When therapist reactions have such pejorative meaning, personal disclosure for the practitioner, and perhaps even a sense of personal openness to the disclosures of others, looms as a cautious if not neglected enterprise. Disclosure becomes fraught with fears of lack of professionalism and needless professional guilt, not only in regard to the views of one's colleagues but in relations to one's own judgments as well. Even for the therapist who intellectually favors self-disclosure and the proper place of therapist feelings in psychotherapy, the actual exercise of this theoretical stance renders the therapist vulnerable to criticism. This everyday conflict for the practicing clinician must to some extent be attributable to the ambience of the profession in its entirety—a troublesome artifact of the struggles of a profession which still suffers lingering but unnecessary doubt concerning its scientific merit.

Yet a third basis for the denial of power is related to the negative aura surrounding therapist feelings: i.e., members of the psychotherapy profession try to preserve a highly positive if not idealized view of therapists. Some clinicians, as Balint (1951) points out in his reflections on the field, want to see themselves as resolved and free from the conflicts and troubles of the *hoi polloi*, the common persons who appear in psychological clinics as clients. Supposedly exempt from worrisome concerns, these clinicians purport to respond with unbroken objectivity and clarity of vision; their position leaves little chance for the introduction of inadmissible feelings like power or hostility, which of course would contradict such a positive image.

Among other thoughtful writers, Winnicott (1949) is emphatic about therapists' attempts to deny difficult feelings such as unambivalent hate.[4] As this paper implies, the idealization of a therapist reflects the very power feelings it is intended to conceal and further exacerbates the problem of professional avoidance of open appraisal.

Lastly, the pronounced emphasis on the client's personality in psychotherapy represents the most apparent reason for denial. Ordinarily, much is written in professional journals and popular accounts concerning the fears of the client, the problems of the client, or the perceptions of the client. The client's inner life is rightly the central concern of any psychotherapy, but too often this single-minded concentration reflects therapists' defensive attempts to deter criticism. Therapists sometimes develop an "I'm okay, you're sick" attitude and psychotherapies suffer enormously as a result. Such therapists expend little effort in reviewing their own contributions and attribute nearly all problems to the condition of the client. Therapists may shun mutuality and maintain dominance at a considerable cost, as they deny and subordinate their own feelings and distort those of their clients.

These four general factors take more defined shape in regard to the specific denial of power feelings, about which strikingly little is written. For instance, the traditionally negative connotation assigned to power, like the aforementioned negative view of therapist feelings, is a primary cause in the widespread neglect of power. In a cogent discussion of power as an impasse in psychotherapy, therapist William Gadpaille (1972) comments:

> In analytic terms, power is a dirty word whether one has it or doesn't, accepts it or repudiates it. The weight of analytic writing, [however minimal], remains opposed to the exercise of anything that might be considered power by the analyst. . . . The analyst is envisioned as solely an enabler in the maturation of the analysand's ego, and this function is somehow not perceived as the exercise of power. (p. 175)

While Gadpaille addressed the practice of psychoanalysis, his astute observations might well apply to other approaches as well. The client-centered school, which we shall examine in closer detail in a later chapter, speaks in an even more vociferous fashion about its anti-power philosophy and approach to psychotherapy.

In addition to such considerations that are true for other therapist feelings besides power, several other tendencies related to power help explain its denial. We can understand these tendencies as a triad of therapist concerns: the fear of influence; the fear of recognizing the limitations of influence; and the fear of struggling with the complexities and anxieties associated with decisions of influence.

The fear of influence results in professional difficulty when therapists openly argue that their impact is minimal while their therapy experiences indicate otherwise. For a child psychotherapist who is helping to shape the growth of a youngster, the inherent power in affecting the child's personality may seem scary and worrisome. Thus therapists do not acknowledge the power—even to themselves. Yet, with a severely troubled child, a therapist can even become something of a surrogate parent who very much influences the life course of the child. In such a situation, which is far from uncommon in child psychotherapy, therapist power is extensive but difficult to translate into a language that is understandable and acceptable in the professional literature.

Ironically, while there is a reluctance to affirm the nature and degree of power when it is apparent, clinicians show a comparable reserve concerning the boundaries of influence. The position of therapist is ripe for the omnipotent strivings of the practitioner and therapists can be vulnerable to inflated views of themselves. To discuss and investigate the limitations of power would mean relinquishing such strivings, however unmentioned or unconscious they may be. To address the boundaries of influence would also mean admitting to certain feelings of powerlessness in treating a dying geriatrics patient, for example, or acknowledging the quagmires in treating a client who brings forth the therapist's own neurotic tendencies. Accepting a realistic range of power feelings or their absence is not easy for therapists, as with the layperson, since such acceptance intimately touches upon professional self-conception.

Therapists also seem to deny power to avoid trying to unravel its complexities—the healing potential of power as well as the abusive potential. When therapists alleviate or exacerbate psychological turmoil, then they indeed hold great power in relation to individual clients. To encounter this issue reality demands unusual concentration and introspection. In fact, therapists even seem to experience ambivalence about recognizing and acknowledging beneficent applications of power. The profession as a whole does not always explicitly honor such individual efforts and therapeutic contributions. Kenneth Clark, in his presidential address at the American Psychological Association Convention in 1971, which he ironically entitled *The Pathos of Power* in reference to the political concerns of the historical times, voiced concern about the profession's fear of power and established a fundamental task for his colleagues: "As a discipline, we need to understand and control the tendencies of those having access to vast resources to submerge their uniquely human, moral and ethical characteristics out of a fear of power" (Clark, 1971).

As we move to the existing literature concerning therapist reactions, it is important to recognize that the relative neglect of power in no way diminishes its importance for the field or for clinical practice. In psychotherapy, it seems, what initially emerges as an oversight often with enhanced consideration develops into an essential area for understanding and for action.

THERAPIST REACTIONS IN THE LITERATURE

The effort to understand the reactions of psychotherapists coincides with the attempts to define the specific term "countertransference." This effort has been as highly elusive and frustrating an endeavor as the history of psychotherapy and psychoanalysis has yet demonstrated. In a composite historical review written 30 years ago, psychoanalyst Douglas Orr (1954) surmised: "There is almost universal agreement on the crucial importance of countertransference, but far from unanimous agreement on how the concept is to be understood" (p. 668).

Today, these words have not lost a certain truthfulness. Therapist reactions remain controversial and are subject to several conflicting perspectives, each trying to explain their nature and place in psychotherapy. A most enduring influence in the everyday practices of psychotherapists, if not also for the scholarly literature, these three approaches seem to encompass the wide variety of therapist reactions. While the three current conceptions of therapist reactions suggest divergent and independent directions for the individual therapist, they also reflect the evolutionary path the profession has traced: from a circumscribed domain to a virtually limitless spectrum of therapist contributions. The conceptions of therapist reaction are known as "the classical," "the objective," and "the totalistic" stances, respectively.

The "classical" view of countertransference interprets the concept most narrowly. Ushered in with Sigmund Freud's admonition "to recognize and overcome this countertransference" (Freud, 1910)[5], the classical interpretation defines a therapist reaction as the residual neurosis of the therapist which promotes departure from therapeutic neutrality. The feelings associated with such a reaction are considered "inappropriate" or "distorted" derivatives of the therapist's unconscious past rather than the psychotherapeutic present.

Therapist reactions are not considered a relevant part of the current psychotherapy with a patient. Expressed more colorfully, the classical view might further suggest that therapist reactions "introduce an accidental casting of the analyst in the psychoanalytic drama" (Gitelson, 1962, p. 194). The sources of such obstructions are considered quite numerous by classicists, who see these sources as multidetermined and as varied as the range of psychological difficulties allow.

The classical perspective is characterized by its repeated emphasis on the dangers of therapist feelings and their expression. Among other negative effects they cite, classicists argue that therapist feelings obscure such basic processes as empathy and understanding (Reich, 1966; Fliess, 1953). The major premise implicit in these concerns may be stated as follows: when therapists are marching to the pressing sound of their own needs, they cannot attend to the beat of their clients' communications, particularly those unconscious messages that require a most perspicacious attention.

While prohibiting open expression of feeling by the therapist, the classical view also addresses more subtle countertransference abuses. For example, therapists who react to the dream of a client might concentrate on their own associations rather than those of the client. In lucid contrast to its ample recognition of negative implications, the classical approach does not acknowledge a role for the beneficial application of therapist reactions and thus does not contribute to the literature in that behalf.

With regard to issues of power, the classical orientation underscores the therapist's "power over countertransference," i.e., the obligation to manage his or her own affective state in order to render it unobtrusive (Ferenczi, 1919). Early accounts of the mishandling and mismanagement of feelings sound nearly evangelical, as if depicting a classical struggle against the destructive forces of countertransference.

Although a few exceptions do appear in the literature, explicit references to power feelings are rare among classical papers. Among these scarce offerings, several articles concerning the narcissism of the therapist refer to insatiable feelings of power, but unfortunately, provide little substantive elaboration (Fenichel, 1941). When an author examines particular neurotic styles, therapist power may be discussed under the heading of "arrogance of the clinician" or "aggressive posture" (Azorin, 1957). More recently, these few writings suggest an increasing interest in the moralistic attitudes of therapists, particularly those attitudes that are related to theoretical orientation. For certain, the topic of morality and power deserves more concerted attention (Langs, 1976).

Despite its limited scope, the classical approach offers an initial and enduring breakthrough into the world of therapist reactions. Most importantly, it suggests that therapists too, along with their clients, introduce a personal element into psychotherapy and may indeed affect therapeutic outcome as a result. Yet the approach implies that both therapist and client are self-enclosed, insular systems rather than interacting participants in the same system, and thus it contributes very little concerning therapeutic interaction.

Robert Langs, a major proponent of an interactionist view

of psychotherapy, speaks to the classical oversights and their significance: "To truly appreciate what is going on intrapsychically we must first know what is happening interactionally" (1976, p. 111). The classical view also fails to link countertransference and the presence of anxiety for both parties in the clinical situation. Additionally, it refrains from addressing the possible relationship between therapist reactions and therapist resistance (Wolstein, 1959). With reference to power, this portion of the literature does not discuss the determinants of power nor does it intimate how power may influence therapist activity.

In total, the classical interpretation of countertransference is inconsistent. While it depicts an unrealistic and static therapist, with a small number of unresolved concerns, at the same time it emphasizes a dynamic and realistic picture of the client and the client's unfolding saga.

The "objective" view represents a decided transition in perspective from the classical view. Rather than concentrate on the pathological or neurotic contributions of the therapist, the objective approach focuses upon the characteristic problems of the client and their impact upon the feelings of the therapist. By concentrating on this sector of interpersonal discourse alone, the objective view defines countertransference in a relatively narrow conception: a therapist's typical and expected response to the evocative behavior of a client or, in other terms, the feelings of the therapist that correspond to the role he or she is placed in by a client. As an illustration, we can imagine a withdrawn and taciturn client who leaves a therapist feeling bored, restless, and uninvested in the psychotherapeutic task.

Wilhelm Reich's approach to psychotherapy, "character analysis," may well have provided the impetus for the objective stance with its own emphasis on typologies of clients. Reich was one of the first therapists to take notes on his personal reactions and to attend seriously to the relationship between client style and therapist style (Wolstein, 1959). In offering this contribution, Reich was attempting to make the vast array of client difficulties more sensible and less confusing to the psychotherapists of his era.

According to the therapeutic framework envisioned by the objective view, a therapist appears as a technical recorder of significant information concerning the personality of the client. Therapists must monitor their reactions for feedback about their clients, and then must secondarily allow the processing of knowledge to inform their interventions.

At times, therapists may want to avoid or rid themselves of noxious or unpleasant feelings, such as anger or jealousy. At other times, they may not be able to account for their current feelings. Particularly at such moments, according to the objective view, therapists must scrutinize their responses for clues to the clients' inner states, or in some cases, the client's dynamic history. In the extreme objective position, the feelings of interest are only those made understandable to the therapist through an appreciation of the client.

With regard to the overall literature, the objective perspective introduces the notion that a therapist reaction can be an advantageous clinical tool. This idea suggests that therapists learn more about clients than they sometimes realize and hence amass a virtual encyclopedia of information about a client. More to the point, the content of a therapist's reaction may be a diagnostic indicator (Kohut, 1968; Balint & Balint, 1939) or a means for comprehending the ongoing process between the participants (Tauber, 1954). Some objective-oriented clinicians suggest that therapist reactions represent a kind of analogue to the responses of significant others in the life of the client (Greenson, 1967).

Relative to the classical view, the objective perspective offers a few insights into the phenomenon of power in psychotherapy. Even with this objective view, however, power is still by no means a focal or common concern. When power is obliquely addressed, it appears in clinical vignettes with selected types of clients. Further discussion of such examples appear in a later chapter on personality sources of power, but a brief listing of significant papers which relate to power may be helpful. These illustrations are listed by client populations that are central to their discussions:

1. Schizophrenic inpatients (Searles, 1958)
2. Borderline inpatients and outpatients (Adler & Buie, 1972; Kernberg, 1965)

3. Character disorder clients, especially those who seem unusually helpless (Giovacchini, 1978)
4. Narcissistic personality clients (Kernberg, 1970; Kohut, 1968)
5. Neurotic clients with unusual separation-individuation difficulties (Kahn, 1969)

In summarizing this second of the three primary approaches to therapist reactions, it seems that the objective view provides more of an interpersonal outlook on psychotherapy while not truly recognizing the more individual contributions of the therapist. Therefore, it does not distinguish between obstructive or constructive contributions. Feeling reactions, whether those of the therapist or those of the client, are examined in the objective view for only their possible pathological and inappropriate presence. The objective position, like its classical predecessor, fails to address the possible realistic and necessary place of such reactions as power in the ongoing psychotherapy relationship.

The "totalistic" approach to therapist reactions, the most recent inductee into the literature, concentrates upon all the feelings and thoughts of the therapist as experienced in relation to a particular psychotherapy[6] The totalistic view combines those pathologically-induced or role-related reactions suggested by the classical and objective definitions. In addition, this newer conception includes within its purview all other therapist feelings that occur as a result of the clinical situation. The quintessential premise of the totalistic view is that a therapist reacts fully, both emotionally and cognitively, to the actual person of the client, and further, that this reactivity profoundly affects the course of psychotherapy.

The current and realistic responses of the therapist first became an imminent concern during the 1950s, when the opaqueness and neutrality of a therapist became a subject of considerable controversy (e.g., see Little, 1957; Racker, 1957; Orr, 1954). More recently, the totalistic interpretation has shown a resurgence of interest largely as a result of trends within psychoanalytic psychology, trends which stress a genuine or real relationship between therapist and client (Greenson, 1967). Transitions within the field overall, such as the increased attention to "here and now" experiencing in the gestalt and encounter group approaches to psychotherapy (Perls, 1973), have also exerted their respective influences.

Given its contemporary origins, the totalistic perspective includes a wide variety of previously underacknowledged therapist experiences. A sample of these therapist reactions include the following therapist qualities: warmth and basic liking (Bordin, 1973; Rogers, 1967); determination (Money-Kyrle, 1957); responsibility (Little, 1957); satisfaction (Szasz, 1956); and empathy (Rogers, 1967, among many others). From the totalistic perspective, such feelings interact with other therapist characteristics and moods to create a complex emotional field for both the therapist and the client.

Clearly, the totalistic view of therapist reactions places greatest importance on the interpersonal nature of psychotherapy. While noting the unique humanness of the therapist, the perspective also proposes a dynamic and constant interaction between the therapist and client in the psychotherapeutic setting (Alger, 1966). It seems that both participants bring their strengths as well as their vulnerabilities to the clinical situation; how these personalities work together will determine in large part the significant reactions each will experience. According to the totalistic conception, this interplay may be unconscious as well as conscious; communication may be intrapsychic as well as interpersonal (Brockbank, 1970; Nacht, 1965).

With respect to reactions of power, totalistic writers are quite sensitive to a therapist's potential for impact with a client. While it has not yet addressed the occurrence of power reactions in any concentrated way, the totalistic view makes a few noteworthy contributions. Some papers on specific client types are now adopting a more interpersonal focus and attending to recurrent therapist-client patterns (e.g., Kernberg, 1970). Other theoretical articles indicate an implicit interest in power with regard to the sense of reality and personal values that a therapist communicates (Novey, 1966), in relation to the advocation of cultural values and norms (Spiegel, 1959), and in relation to the implementation of standards and prohibitions (Weisman, 1972). As with the classical and objective approaches, however, the totalistic approach has yet to inspire empirical investigation of therapist reactions in general or of power in particular.

Nonetheless, such a comprehensive effort as the totalistic perspective begins to eradicate the negative stigma previously placed on therapist feelings and illuminates the process of psychotherapy for closer examination. At the same time that it provides an opportunity for finer classification of therapist reactions, the totalistic view directs greater attention to the realistic aspects of psychotherapy, particularly those ingredients of therapy that may be crucial for personality change. Additionally, the totalistic view suggests new pathways for more extensive consideration, e.g., the effects of intercurrent life events like pregnancy or illness[7] on client behavior (Cohen, 1952). In essence, this totalistic understanding of therapist reactions has greatest utility precisely because it best captures the inner emotional life of the therapist in psychotherapy.

BEYOND THE DENIAL OF POWER

Despite the contributions made by a variety of authors, none of these several perspectives offers a thorough analysis of the power reactions of psychotherapists. Even the youngest of the three views, the totalistic, has only begun to address particular therapist reactions such as power. This oversight is still apparent despite the very inclusive definition of therapist reactions offered by the totalistic approach.

Thus, what is required is a deeper and more comprehensive inquiry into the nature of individual reactions like power using a totalistic looking-glass as a medium for inquiry. With the chapters that follow, I hope to make a significant inroad in this undertaking—to refine our appreciation of power in psychotherapy in the way that other reactions might be similarly considered. The domain of interest, as is perhaps by now quite apparent, reflects all the power reactions of a therapist—be they conscious or unconscious, realistic responses or fictitious distortions, elements of the past or moments of the living present.

II. SOURCES OF POWER

SOURCES OF POWER

"Sources of power" are the foundations on which therapist powers are based. The succeeding three chapters consider the many origins of therapist power—the ascribed powers inherent in the culture, the varied powers built into the institution of psychotherapy, and ultimately, the respective powers endemic to the therapist and client as individuals.

Cultural expectations, as discussed in Chapter 3, are important for therapist power because they provide the context in which psychotherapy takes place. Equally important is the fact that cultural considerations dictate the roles assigned to a given position like the therapist's (Rowan, 1976). These roles are a set of normative characteristics that prescribe and proscribe therapist behavior. Thus, cultural considerations help to establish areas of therapist power and the multitude of behaviors that may follow from such power.

The social institution of psychotherapy assumes power from the culture and channels it through its various treatment approaches and theories of technique. In Chapter 4, we concentrate on perhaps the three best known approaches in order to decipher their power components. Concerning the institutional level, we attend to the socialization and training of power, role definitions within each school, and designated tasks and purposes within each approach. Eventually, organizational or institutional planning gives way to actual therapist behaviors; we cite some of the recurrent practices of each of the three schools.

The decidedly interpersonal nature of psychotherapy insures that individual personality will be a prominent source of power. Personality seems a basic factor in the appearance of power. Political observer Harold Lasswell, in an analysis of the motives and attributes of world leaders, argues that power and personality are inseparably linked on a global political level (Lasswell, 1955). Despite the massive impact of culture and institutions, personality and the relationship among personalities represent the final echelon in a process of power distillation. In Chapter 5, we examine the role of therapist and client personality characteristics and social status characteristics in the creation of therapist power.

Several background properties of power sources should be mentioned here. First, the types of sources (cultural, institutional, interpersonal) are not wholly independent of each other. For instance, the power that accompanies the ability to comfort may be both culturally-determined and personality-determined for a given therapist. Secondly, one level of power sources (e.g., institutional) tends to filter power which may originate from another source (e.g., cultural). Thus, the power of knowledge, a cultural power, is translated in the psychoanalytic interpretation or the client-centered response, which are institutionally bestowed powers. Finally, power may be socialized directly and need not pass through all the levels of power. For example, the sometimes ineffable powers of the therapeutic relationship often seem to have little obvious cultural origin; the primary socializing agents would be the institutional and interpersonal realms of power.

Chapter 3

CULTURAL SOURCES
The Powers That Be

Cultural expectations about power can profoundly influence an individual. Characteristic roles and attributes related to these roles, assigned by a culture to a particular position like that of "psychotherapist," play no small part in the development of power. In *Power and the Two Revolutions*, Daniel Yankelovich (1972) speaks to the impact of a changing cultural-historical ambience on those who seek psychotherapy:

> With respect to therapy, many observers have noted that the tensions of the society do carry over to the types of patients analysts see in their offices. . . .Erikson notes that the classic cases of hysteria which loomed so large in Freud's practice have virtually disappeared. In the 1950s and '60s analysts saw many patients, especially younger ones, whose central concern related to the quest for a surer sense of personal identity. Today, the themes of power and powerlessness and how the individual can find a satisfactory life for himself in this society are likely to appear with increasing frequency. (p. 102)

This historical motif concerning power and powerlessness would seem to be continuing in the 1980s, when the threat of global extinction and the decline of individualism loom as rampant concerns. If such fluctuations in the mindset of western culture do indeed shape the difficulties of individual clients entering therapy, then perhaps cultural beliefs and trends pattern the power concerns of individual therapists. The idea is compelling even when one sets aside the contemporary fascination with power.

Since the inception of psychotherapy, western culture has conferred upon therapists a number of prototypal roles and certain special powers related to these roles. These cultural assignments are sources of power based on popular expectations. As members of the larger culture, therapist and client personally introduce these common expectations into the clinical setting.

CULTURAL ROLES

The Doctor Role

The historical relationship between medicine and psychotherapy instills an expectation concerning medical care into the image of a psychotherapist. Not only an implicit role created by practitioners and clients, the doctor role is a relatively clear and explicit role that stands on the educational overlap between medicine and psychology. It also rests on common terminology and on similar conceptions of therapeutic tasks. This overlap is particularly true for disease-oriented approaches to psychotherapy.

It is difficult to imagine a psychotherapist who does not function in some way as a doctor. The nature of the profession, with its emphasis on psychological aid to those in pain, seems to demand that a practitioner assume a doctor role. Whatever the theoretical predilections of a given therapist, the basic scenario of psychotherapy is nearly universal: a troubled, suffering individual who comes to a professional in search of relief from current living circumstances; this person depends upon the professional for help and for amelioration of these circumstances.

Clients seek a healing and reparative service and the therapist is expected to perform that function. Despite individual differences in approach the role of doctor endures.

The doctor role is a decidedly powerful one. In contemporary western culture, doctors undeniably have tremendous impact on the way society thinks about health and the quality of life; because of their close relationship to the medical profession, psychotherapists do, too. Thus, a psychotherapist symbolizes health and assumes a gatekeeper function in terms of health.

In essence, the therapist becomes the guardian of psychological well-being. Since personal psychology is so sensitive an area and its healthy maintenance so basic, the psychotherapist becomes an unusually significant figure as a client's troubles and maladies become prominent. Moreover, the inherent dependency of the psychotherapeutic relationship ensures that a therapist presides over the well-being of the client. Therapist and client preserve intact, in some respects exaggeratedly, the traditional features of dependency and power of the physician-patient relationship (Stone, 1961).

The Scientist/Expert Role

Western culture also defines a therapist as a technical and scientific expert. In caricature, the therapist emerges as something of a psychological "answer-man" who reduces all problems or quandaries to their logical causes.

In the tradition of Charcot and Freud, therapists possess an understanding of the sometimes hidden and powerful forces that are at the center of an individual. If their orientation is psychoanalytic, they assiduously implement their analytic skills in the laboratory of the unconscious. If their inclination is behavioral, they adopt a variety of action-oriented techniques and apply their craft in the realm of overt behavior. In either case, the culture demands a scientist/expert who applies observations and discoveries to the problems of current life situations.

A psychotherapist acts as an expert when offering informed explanations for previously inexplicable and troublesome phenomena. Relying on a combination of professional training and native aptitude, or perhaps more appropriately "intuition," the therapist formulates clinical hypotheses concerning a vast array of presenting concerns. Sometimes, as is often the case with unusual problems like anorexia or agoraphobia (i.e., fear of leaving the home), a client's behavior may be nearly incomprehensible to the layperson. Yet even with regard to more common difficulties like neurotic depression, a therapist derives substantial power.

The culture and its individuals look to the psychotherapist as a professional for a more complex explanation of the nuances of a disorder. Today, western culture seems to rely more and more on specialization in such professional fields as psychotherapy for improvements in everyday living. Psychotherapy and psychotherapists, by attempting to satisfy this expectation, occupy an increasingly influential position among other callings in science and education that address comparable issues (Bromberg, 1962).

Focal to the therapeutic process, psychotherapists rely upon a clinical method like the scientific method. Initially, a therapist collects observations and ventures hypotheses about an individual. He or she frequently considers a number of alternative possibilities and then assesses the validity of these inferences in clinical interaction, commonly using the client's reaction as the litmus test for the inferences. For purposes of classification, the therapist applies technical concepts and language, a kind of shorthand notation not unlike chemical formulae. Such exclusive and cryptic language enhances the power of the professional, who joins the small coterie for whom phrases like "oral-depressive core" or "stress response syndrome" have meaning. The client must turn to the clinical expert to decipher the language of personality just as the layperson must look to the chemist to simplify the terminology of that science.

These expert and scientific functions create the opportunity for considerable power, but are unfortunately prone to professional abuses of power. Indeed, psychotherapists can sometimes become such staunch enthusiasts of their own theories that they lose sight of the fallibilities of a particular view. In the most alarming of scenarios, a therapist might impose a professed expertise and influence coercively and unrealistically, thus weaving self-centered interests into an intellectual stance. In speaking about the history of the scientific process, in a fashion that may well apply to the specific discipline of psychology, philosopher Charles Baudoin (1923) observes:

> Theories dominate the mind in so far as they are accepted; they can exercise their full power upon the feeling and the imagination. (p. 33)

In psychotherapy, however, it is quite apparent that a certain conviction in one's professional merit is essential for effective and consistent treatment. What all this suggests is that the power of science and expertise may be just as potentially abusive as it is therapeutically necessary.

The Parent Role

The popular cartoonlike conception of a therapist, a bearded, rotund figure exuding complacency and flourishing a turn-of-the-century pipe, exemplifies the culture's need for a parental figure and probably a paternal one at that. While individual therapists vary greatly in their similarity to this incarnation, the culture expects that a therapist will present a parental image and assume a caretaking manner. In addition to the great shadow left by patriarchs like Freud, the nature of psychotherapy itself contributes to the parental role associated with psychotherapists.

Inevitably, a therapist is perceived by a client as a supplier of provisions, psychological supplies that are sought after for socio-emotional health. Like a parent seen through the eyes of a child, the therapist often represents a dispenser of affection, confirmation, support, and love. Many therapists do provide some psychological sustenance, yet much of the power of therapists comes from their clients' wishes for nurturance and their clients' belief that the therapists will satisfy these wishes.

The parental analogy is not based on the bestowing of positive regard and nurturance alone. Therapists are also asked to work as "limit setters," very much the way a parent offers structure for a young child. Thus, a client may seek help in organizing a personal life in a manner similar to the way parents organize the sometimes confusing small worlds of children. Psychoanalytic psychotherapy, for example, depends upon the relationship between parental and therapeutic limit setting to reconstruct a client's early emotional relationship to structure (Bieber, 1972; Dince, 1972).

The literature on the inherent power of the parental role is voluminous. Developmental psychologist Lois Hoffman summarizes the prevailing view when she comments: "Probably in no other relationship does a person in our society have such complete power over another as do parents over young children" (1960). Studies of parental influence factors (Rollins & Thomas, 1975, for example) provide supporting evidence of the importance of power issues in caretaking behavior.

The Guide Role

Contemporary culture also asks a therapist to act as guide for the educational or psychological dimensions of a client's life. The therapist may even become a spiritual facilitator. Culturally, we see the therapist as leading a client to an as yet unforeseen destination. The therapist serves as a sagacious companion who offers fresh observations yet allows the client to independently choose among pathways to follow.

A therapist who serves as a guide becomes a highly valued and powerful person in the eyes of a client. Though their relationship is transitional, the impact of the therapist on the client can be lifelong. Therapist Sheldon Kopp (1972) offers this caveat about the responsibility inherent in the role: "If the realm in which this power is to be realized is turned toward the creative possibilities of the self, then excitement or joy becomes possible. But if this freedom is experienced as power over others, both parties will be trapped".[1] As Kopp suggests, awareness of culturally assigned roles tends to acquaint a therapist with the nature and limitations of power.

Power concerns are inherent in the guide role and place it as the most controversial of the various therapist roles. The need for a guide figure (sometimes pejoratively called a "guru figure" by its critics) elicits consternation from some in the profession of psychotherapy. Those who oppose the notion of a guide role feel that psychotherapy strays too far afield from the discipline of science and too closely toward religion. In contrast, others see the guide role as important if not necessary for successful intensive psychotherapy, a response to the needs of a developing individual for someone who can facilitate the rites of growth. This view is supported by the life span research of Levinson et al (1978). In *Seasons of a Man's Life*, Levinson and his colleagues emphasize the importance of a mentor or guide figure as a transition to adulthood.

It may be that the guide role is therapeutic when, like other mentor relationships, it allows the client substantially greater freedom. When it compensates for a client's fear of independence and growth, however, then it betrays its essential purpose: to prepare the way for life's journey.

In summarizing the place of the guide role in relation to the other therapist roles, psychologist and Episcopal priest William Crosby offers an interesting overview:

> The role of the psychotherapist can be understood on a number of levels. If the focus is on the symptoms, then the therapist is a kind of technician. If the focus is on the dynamics, then the therapist works with his own personality by withholding or expressing it in the relationship. . . . At the level of faith, the therapist is a companion and guide facilitating the journey from fear to love, from an inner world (and by projection, an outer world) that, to some degree, is in shadow and darkness into a world characterized by light. (Stern, 1981, p. 118)

CULTURAL POWERS

By virtue of the confluence of these several roles, our culture grants to a therapist powers within particular domains. These domains include a cross-section of five areas, ranging from the most technical of concerns to the most personal. All of these therapist powers may precede the beginning of psychotherapy for the participants. While some anticipated power is realistic, other power is less realistic and indicative of the fantasy wishes of society and of the participants. What follows is a description of these realms of cultural power.

The Power of Knowledge

Paramount among culturally ascribed realms of power is the power of knowledge.[2] Developing out of the scientist, doctor, and parent roles, a therapist is believed to be an intellectually resourceful and even an omniscient figure.

In view of the culture, a therapist accrues power through scholarship in theoretically-based psychology, and often in conjunction with formal schooling and systematic study. He or she derives further power by demonstrating expert knowledge of the therapy process. The therapist may also convey a perspicacity about the sequencing of events in the course of therapy, a capacity to know when the process is off course, or a reliability for informed prediction. Of healers far and wide, Frank (1973) comments on the importance of prediction and its impact on perceived power:

> [Among others] Shamans are usually adept at distinguishing illnesses they can treat successfully from those that are beyond their powers. This enables them to maintain a reputation for success which . . . undoubtedly enhances their healing power. (p. 156)

The culture thus attributes a kind of special wisdom to its therapists. We expect that a therapist will have had a variety of rich personal life experiences and will therefore be able to enlighten the experiences of others. In conjunction with the guide role, we anticipate a unique sensitivity to hidden connections and an unusual ability to perceive relationships among complex phenomena.[3] Believing in the therapist's wisdom, clients naturally look to the therapist for insights and answers.

Whose Life Is It Anyway? (1978), a tragicomedy written by Brian Medoff, provides a graphic illustration of power derived from knowledge in the health fields. Concerned with the right to determine one's own medical fate, the play traverses the health professions and medical care practices in its indictment of practitioner/patient relations. In one memorable scene, the presiding physician, Dr. Emerson, defends his decision to sustain his quadriplegic patient: "My power isn't arbitrary; I've earned it, with knowledge and skill and it's also subject to the laws of nature."

Even when circumstances are less extreme, it seems, these powers of knowledge and skill can be unimaginably vast, particularly as they touch upon issues of life and death, sanity and insanity. Sometimes our culture is quite willing to grant such power to its health professionals and it becomes incumbent upon the professional, if he or she chooses to accept, to exert such power.

The Power of Faith

Arising from the parent, guide, and doctor roles, the power of faith implies that a therapist's expectancies can be powerful in themselves and may be influential in therapeutic outcome. A therapist who exudes hope may be able to invigorate or catalyze healing motives with a client. One reflecting therapist explains why the culture requires faith from a therapist:

> Often the people who come for therapy have lost faith in themselves; beset with problems and armored with defenses, the client cannot see much positive potential. The faith of the therapist in seeing what the person can be plants a powerful seed for the person's own potentialities. (Stern, 1981, p. 130)

A therapist attains power as he or she communicates that life circumstances can ultimately improve. As this reality suggests, clients frequently enter psychotherapy in a beleaguered state and need the therapist to confront their despair; perhaps faith in the possibility for change may combat the hopelessness of circular, self-defeating patterns of living.

While our culture turns to therapists for optimism about improvement, it also expects them to convey in convincing fashion that the power for change resides in the therapist's office. The therapist may also express confidence in the individual client and base this view on knowledge of the client's history and strengths. Thus, faith must be tempered with a sense of informed conviction about the individual. The culture provides the therapist with the power to offer faith and reason for the immediate present, and this may well be vital for a client. The expression of faith seems to be an integral part of therapy and some therapists even feel it is essential for a positive outcome (Schulman, 1964).

The form by which faith is communicated will vary from therapy to therapy. A therapist may express a certain confidence in a client based on the client's history and personal strengths. The culture provides the therapist with an implicit power to offer such faith in the client in the immediate present. In other therapy circumstances, such as psychotherapy with a potentially suicidal patient, the therapist conveys faith (as well as protection) by personal investment and physical presence.

In some downtrodden conditions, where verbal psychotherapy is not tenable, some degree of faith may be restored in the client through pharmacological treatment. Here, in particular, the importance of the faith of the therapist as a catalyst for client hopefulness cannot be overstated. Numerous drug studies have substantiated the importance and power of therapist expectations (including faith in the treatment) on resulting drug efficacy (Frank, 1973; Uhlenhuth, 1959).

With regard to pharmacological methods, it seems that therapeutic interventions gain greatest potency through their symbolic power in addition to their actual chemical action. According to Frank (1973), in a summary of the related literature on drug effects, a therapist's faith in a drug seems to activate client expectations, which, having a power of their own, alter emotions that influence the sensation of pain. Similarly, Wilkins (1977), in his own compendium of associated studies of expectations in applied settings, concludes that practitioners' beliefs consistently and pervasively influence the outcome of their endeavors.

The Power to Comfort

An age-old derivative of the doctor role and an outgrowth of early parental functions, the power to comfort is expected of therapists from nearly all theoretical backgrounds. Empowered to respond to pain, the therapist faces increasing numbers in our technological age who seek relief from psychological and existential despair (Frank, 1973). The essential sign of this power to deliver others from pain is sometimes called "the healing touch." Based on a popular notion within and outside of psychotherapeutic circles, a healing touch suggests that the manner of some gifted individuals in itself engenders recovery.

The power to comfort is particularly trenchant because people who enter psychotherapy usually do so out of psychic pain. They come looking for relief and for transition to a more tranquil state of living. In *Freud and the Soul*, Bruno Bettelheim (1982) extracts from Freud's essential humanism the nature of therapeutic comfort: " . . . a spontaneous sympathy of our [therapists'] unconscious with that of others, a feeling response of our soul to others" (p. 52). Indeed, the power to comfort often seems implicit in the writings of Freud, just as it implicitly appears in the psychotherapy process and in cultural expectations about psychotherapy.

The Power of Heroism

The culture also sees therapists as heroic or even magical to a certain extent. Heroic power is a less frequently acknowledged source of power. Related to the doctor and guide roles, and also suggested by the idealized feelings which sometimes accompany parenthood, heroic power refers to the view of a therapist as a savior from life's distress. In the client's perspective or the therapist's own, perhaps the therapist can transform the abyss of suffering into a world of happiness. Concerning the historical roots of this magical notion, Spanish psychologist Carlos Sequin (1965) writes:

> Let us remember that the first psychotherapists were the priests and magicians of prescientific cultures who acted as representatives of or vehicles for the supernatural powers to which the desperate patient would have recourse. . . . When psychotherapy began to be practiced by the doctor, it preserved to a degree its magical significance, which, whether one likes it or not, was incorporated into the art of medicine. (p. 67)

Applied to the individual therapist, the power of heroism is often though not always unrealistic. Clients frequently invoke heroic fantasies out of wishes for an early omnipotent figure. It is not difficult to imagine a client who expects that a therapist will magically change the whole course of life—the past and the future as well as the present. Such a client searches for someone who can take care of everything and even undo the family wrongs.

Yet, as Kopp (1978) points out, certain interventions of the therapist, such as interpretations or therapeutic suggestions, can give strength to the belief in such magical power, and even, on occasion, falsely resemble a heroic rescue. This heroic power stems from the apparent ability to give special meaning to apparently meaningless or even absurd patterns of living.

Therapists too can enhance client fantasies through these invisible therapeutic methods and a sometimes disguised therapeutic demeanor, the same kind of therapeutic strategies that are so difficult to research. Nonetheless, perhaps there is a place in psychotherapy for a quiet reality-based heroism. It may be that the "heroics" of a therapist may be dedication and perseverance over time in the face of the client's anguish. As Hillman (1964) points out, the archetype of a healer is, after all, a tireless fighter against death and despair, and this seems naturally to suggest a certain heroic image.

The Power of Intimacy

Anticipated companionship in psychotherapy provides a therapist with a power over the provision of intimacy. The culture imbues a therapist with the responsibility to foster an atmosphere of nonthreatening closeness, one in which clients can reveal themselves and their troubles. Tremendous power and leverage go hand-in-hand with such closeness just as they do with the expression of nurturance outside of the clinical setting (Rollins & Thomas, 1975).

The power of intimacy grows as a therapeutic dyad goes through difficult periods together, particularly if intimacy needs are largely unfulfilled elsewhere for the client. Especially when strife is at hand, clients will tend to become dependent on therapists for close involvement and a sense of "being there." In many therapies, such shared experiences and the bonds that are formed remain unacknowledged. Nonetheless, they certainly influence in important ways the potency of the therapist in the eyes of the client.

Though therapist power tends to grow in crisis situations, it certainly accumulates in relation to the intimacy of ordinary therapeutic discourse. Since the vast majority of psychotherapy clients struggle with some confusion concerning intimacy, however mild that confusion might be, therapists tend to offer a brand of attentive intimacy that many of these clients will have difficulty finding elsewhere, i.e., until some change occurs.

The commonplace sharing of intimate personal detail and opinion would seem to confer unusual power, a power of knowledge as well as a power of intimacy. This unique area, the reality of being privy to the most private of thoughts, represents for practicing psychotherapists an important meeting ground for all of their diverse powers.

CULTURAL BEHAVIORS

Specific powers of the culture are very numerous, including both realistic and unrealistic possibilities. The realms of power are infused with multiple cultural roles and reveal myriad particular powers. The following therapist powers represent some of the most common across the comparative psychotherapies.

Knowledge powers (primarily from the doctor, scientist, and parent roles).

1. The power to define disease and health in any given interaction, or overall.
2. The power to label behavioral and/or nonobservable phenomena.
3. The power to offer explanations for these phenomena.
4. The power to assess reality and the limits of what is realistic.
5. The power to make treatment decisions.

Faith Powers (primarily from the doctor, parent, and guide roles).

1. The power to convey faith in the client's ability to change.
2. The power to convey faith in the client's untapped abilities or potential abilities.
3. The power to communicate faith in the therapeutic process.
4. The power to experience and communicate faith in one's self as a therapist.
5. The power to convey faith in other people and in the vicissitudes of life.

Comfort Powers (primarily from the doctor and parent roles).

1. The power to repair emotional wounds.
2. The power to be supportive.
3. The power to confirm the client in some pursuit.
4. The power to compensate for some specified prior deprivation.
5. The power to ease anxiety or enhance anxiety through interventions.

Heroic Powers (primarily from the doctor, scientist, and guide roles).

1. The power to rescue the client from dire psychological or psychosocial circumstances.
2. The power to point toward a life course or at least to foresee the potential pathways.
3. The power magically to undo family wrongs or at least act in contrast to these.
4. The power to champion creative energies.
5. The power to represent or model a heroic figure.

Intimacy Powers (primarily from the parent and guide roles).

1. The power to create an intimate atmosphere in the therapeutic setting.

2. The power to determine the nature of the intimacy (i.e., friendship vs. only professional relationship, etc.).
3. The power to listen to and explore intimate personal concerns.
4. The power to reveal one's own personal concerns.
5. The power to govern the occurrence of physical comfort between therapist and client.

Each of the culturally-attributed powers interacts with the others to create a strong expectancy of power for the individual therapist.

While cultural ascriptions may influence a client directly, they are often filtered through the various psychotherapy approaches. We now move to this institutional level of analysis. We present the major theories of technique and the sources of power inherent in their training therapist role definitions and significant intervention methods.

Chapter 4

INSTITUTIONAL SOURCES
The Corridors of Power

Beyond cultural sources of power, the institution of psychotherapy itself develops therapist power through its various theories
of technique. While cultural expectations provide certain fundamental powers, these powers are filtered through a variety of
therapeutic frameworks.

Three of the best known perspectives, the psychoanalytic,
the client-centered, and the behavioral, illustrate the power inherent in technique and reflect a wide spectrum of attitudes
toward power. Other theoretical perspectives represent specific
contributions of technique and we attend to these perspectives
for illustrative purposes. In considering models of change, a
central issue becomes: What elements of the respective role definitions, therapeutic strategies, and resulting therapist behaviors
lead to power for a practicing clinician?

THERAPIST ROLES

The Socialization Process

Therapists learn therapeutic roles through psychotherapy
training, a professional socialization which retains distinctive

features of a particular theoretical approach and shares characteristics with the procedures of other approaches. Psychoanalytic training is typically formal, lengthy, and intensive; it ordinarily requires the training therapist to undergo treatment. The
basic teaching method is simply the treatment and close supervision of actual psychotherapy cases. Client-centered and behavioral training tends to be less formal and shorter in duration,
sometimes but not always including a self-treatment adjunct.
Client-centered instruction utilizes role-playing and recorded
case material and emphasizes the development of listening skills
rather than theoretical understanding alone. Behavioral schools
also employ role-playing as well as other in vivo, skill-developing
exercises (e.g., assertiveness modeling).

Regardless of their orientation, most training therapists
receive a mixture of didactic and experimental work. Educational centers include graduate and professional schools, hospi-
tals, treatment centers, university counseling agencies, and, in
the case of psychoanalysis, private societies. While many training
programs familiarize an inchoate therapist with comparative approaches, others offer an almost unilateral concentration if not
indoctrination in a singular notion of the therapist role.[1]

While socializing a therapist into a particular theoretically-
based role, training communicates a sense of power to the novice
in several ways. Training tends to suggest a sense of "psychological completeness," particularly in those training packages that
emphasize personal therapy for the trainee. On psychoanalytic
training, Balint (1951) observes that much power is germinated
by the false notion of freedom from all further conflicts and
neuroses. Belief in such a "supertherapy" may conjure fantasies
of therapist omnipotence. In client-centered training, a corol-
lary would be a therapist's vision of the self as a tireless and
unambivalent dispenser of positive regard.

Secondly, training can support and foster a sense of "cho-
senness." Therapeutic emphasis on such personal qualities as intuition and empathy, along with the relative exclusivity of training opportunities, leads therapists to believe they have special
powers to help other people. Since behavioral approaches tend
to de-emphasize the personal qualities of the therapist, they are
less emphatic concerning this belief. Theodore Reik's maxim

that "psychoanalysts are not made but are born that way" has its subscribers among many nonpsychoanalytic therapists as well (Ekstein, 1969).

Training in the various schools also may inculcate a sense of "group omnipotence," an avowed insistence on the superiority of one's own theoretical perspective. Such a belief stems from fraternal feelings and serves something of a defensive function as it rules out the possible contributions of challenging viewpoints. Through unwillingness to recognize the limitations of an approach, therapists assume unwarranted power for that approach. In its extreme, this phenomenon appears in the psychoanalyst who envisions little use for supportive interventions, the behaviorist who will never acknowledge underlying motives, and the Rogerian who with moral uprightness belittles any notion of therapist-inspired insight.

One of the most vivid descriptions of training and life style appears in Janet Malcolm's descriptive essay concerning psychoanalysis, *The Impossible Profession* (1981). While presenting one therapist's view of a single therapeutic approach, Malcolm captures several themes that seem indicative of the profession as a whole. In reading Malcolm's account of the therapist's life style, the reader is struck by both the veteran and the inchoate therapists' close relationship to the mysteries of the human personality. These therapists describe a sense of developing power as a result of their proximity to knowledge, as well as a paradoxical sense of futility over their intellectual limitations.

Equally apparent, however, are the power struggles peculiar to the socialization process of the psychotherapist. With regard to the more negative side effects of orthodox psychoanalytic training and membership in an analytic society, one of Malcolm's therapist interviewees speaks to the issue of power:

> The real issue was that there was a clique of people at the Institute who fill all the important posts and decide who is to become a training analyst, and there is another clique of people who don't have power and who want it. That's what practically every controversy at our institute is about . . . though it's no different anywhere else. (Malcolm, 1981, p. 74)

Whether or not such power concerns are as widespread as this therapist suggests, it seems that the possible consequences of such internal power concerns are plentiful. Above all, implicit power struggles in a training environment or clinic can spill over into the practice of psychotherapy, leaving the clinical situation vulnerable to inappropriate displays of power.

The Psychoanalytic Role

The psychoanalytic conception of psychotherapy focuses on the "power of insight." The primary function of a therapist is to render the unconscious "conscious"—to locate hidden drives, affects, and fantasy constructions and bring them to the surface of awareness. According to the psychoanalytic view, therapists open themselves to the processes of the unconscious and make these processes known to their patients. The practitioner's role is an adversarial one in that he or she takes a stance which opposes the purely conscious communications of the patient.

However, psychoanalytic therapists also perform a facilitative function as they teach the ways of the unconscious. It is particularly because of their access to underlying meaning that psychoanalytic therapists accumulate so much therapeutic power. Yet the inherent interpersonal power that accompanies the facilitation of insight is not commonly discussed in psychoanalytic writings.

The Client-Centered Role

The "power of transaction" governs in the client-centered approach. As their primary role, client-centered therapists are empowered to reflect the client's true self in a spirit of understanding and unconditional positive regard. They attempt to highlight inner feelings rather than reveal unconscious processes. In so doing, the therapist seeks to provide an atmosphere in which clients comfortably experience their "true self."

The client-centered role is designed to be nonadversarial and facilitative of authentic experiencing, although it leaves open the possibility of disagreement about what constitutes true inner feelings. Within this therapeutic landscape, power is derived largely through reflection of inner feelings and expression of unqualified positive regard.

While psychoanalytic definitions of a psychotherapist overlook power concerns, the client-centered conception explicitly denies the presence of therapist power. Client-centered therapy proponents see their brand of psychotherapy as relatively free of power issues. In reviewing the origins of the client-centered movement, Barton (1974) explains: "[Carl] Rogers first introduced his view of therapy as 'nondirective' (out of a tradition of democratic humanism) because he wanted to move away from any notion of therapist authority or priority of vision" (p. 177).

In apparent opposition to the psychoanalytic theory of technique, the Rogerians try to alleviate any parental or "superego" influence on the client. While maintaining an egalitarian stance in theory, the client-centered role may reveal its own underlying power in practice. The vociferous negation of its presence may actually enhance the effect of manifestations of power that we shall argue are common across the comparative psychotherapies.

The Behavioral Role

A behavioral orientation refers to a set of therapeutic approaches which all employ principles of learning to further therapeutic change (Wolpe, 1971). The approaches concentrate on the "power of action." Central to their role, behavioral therapists wish to change client behavior or teach a mastery of action. The behavioral role is more didactic than adversarial, although the use of such techniques as negative reinforcement indicates something of an oppositional therapeutic relationship.

Behaviorally-oriented therapists tend to be much more forthright than their psychoanalytic or client-centered counterparts concerning their inherent power. Clearly within the auspices of their role, behavioral therapists impact upon environmental contingencies in order to institute change. Thus they acknowledge their power and use it as a therapeutic tool.

Behavioral approaches certainly stand out among comparative perspectives in their open management of power. Consider an example from B. F. Skinner's *Walden Two* (1948). While providing a tour of his behavioristically-oriented community, social planner Frazier exclaims to his visitors, "'Of course I'm not indifferent to power!' (Frazier said hotly) 'And I like to play God! Who wouldn't, under the circumstances?'" (p. 299).

THERAPIST TECHNIQUES

Each of the respective roles is accompanied by designated techniques for change. These techniques may involve facilitation and development of certain interpersonal processes as well as the implementation of articulated intervention strategies.

Within the psychoanalytic theory of technique, the process of free association, the unfolding of "transference" and "resistances" and the primary intervention mode, the interpretation, together form the bedrock of psychotherapy. Within the client-centered approach, the expression of therapist attitudes (e.g., unconditional positive regard) and the use of the "client-centered response" are central to the therapeutic process. Behavioral therapies have as their cornerstone an extensive array of environmental manipulations and action-oriented procedures. An underlying theme throughout this analysis is that each of the three views of psychotherapy applies its theory of technique in order to assume therapeutic power, regardless of their differential emphases. Our interest is in exploring how such power comes about.

Psychoanalytic Techniques

Traditional analytic psychotherapy rests on the process of free association, a procedure in which patients are charged spontaneously to emit whatever rises to consciousness and then to consider its meaning. Free association is the basic means of communication in psychoanalysis and one which empowers the therapist to observe and comment upon any aspect of the patient's presenting material. In keeping with a medical analog, the technique demands that the patient "go under" and relinquish control to the probing therapist. The patient must allow him- or herself to regress and at least temporarily give up over-seeing power to the therapist in order to treat conflictual issues.

While this overseeing capacity is powerful in itself, it also sanctions the therapist to choose and focus upon material as he or she wishes. Thus, the patient is directed toward possible re-pressed material or what the therapist judges to be conflictual content. Most commonly, as Bellak (1961) points out, analytic therapists tend to respond to those associations which concern childhood and thus influence their patients to concentrate upon historical reconstruction.

Emerging during the free association experience, the proc-ess of "transference" is considered to be an important and pow-erful tool for understanding how an individual relates to others. Among analytic therapists, transference refers to the experience of feelings, attitudes, fantasies, and other phenomenological experiences which are inappropriate to the present and repeat early childhood reactions.

As transference unfolds, a patient may rediscover all of the significant human relations of the past which are not otherwise accessible to awareness. As the symbolic embodiment of most of these figures, a therapist tends to assume tremendous power— at the very least, the power of father, mother, and siblings all in combination (Greenson, 1967). Moreover, the appearance of transference in the analytic setting offers the opportunity not only to repeat actual relationships, but the simultaneous chance to pursue fantasied and more benign objects as well (Stone, 1961). At the outset, a therapist frequently represents such an idealized figure.

Along with transference, "resistances" are phenomena expected to arise out of the individual client's neuroses. In the psychoanalytic context, resistances refer to all the unconscious forces within a client which oppose the procedures of psycho-therapeutic work and its various tasks (Greenson, 1967; Freud, 1912). The therapist's power indicated by resistance is perhaps less obvious than the power that is part and parcel of the trans-ference experience.

Resistance clearly involves an attempt by the client, however concealed, to maintain power against the real or imagined im-pact of the therapist. In bringing resistances into the limelight,

the therapist assumes greater power through the analysis of resistance. In anticipating the client's apparent efforts to thwart
growth, the therapist claims as a special prerogative the authori-
zation to interpret resistances; even prior to interpretation, it is
the therapist who designates what is or is not a resistance. Such a
conclusive privilege is particularly powerful because it defines a
therapist's interpretive range as exceptionally vast, and it allows
exploration deep inside the client's phenomenal world.

Against the backdrop of free association and the development of transference and resistances, the interpretation is the
most powerful mode of intervention in psychoanalytic psychotherapy. While other types of intervention may appear more
frequently, the interpretation is still the decisive and ultimate
instrument of the analytic therapist (Greenson, 1967; Fromm-
Reichman, 1950). As a means of intervention, the interpretation
embodies the power of the therapist in a number of ways. Above
all, interpretations help to demonstrate a therapist's power to
understand the unconscious. With an interpretation, the therapist can point out how the patient's decision to remain in a pro-
saic relationship stems from early childhood fears of separation.
Secondly, by access to the unconscious, interpretations define
the therapist as the "knower" and as the "dispenser of knowledge" in the treatment situation. Finally, as Stone (1961) observes, interpretations have a great deal of primary transference
weight since their impact is often linked with the deep-seated
effects of early childhood discovery. A psychoanalytic therapist
thus has power related to the patient's natural sense of curiosity
and motivation for learning.

Client-Centered Techniques

While psychoanalytic procedures concentrate on the power
of technical processes, the client-centered approach emphasizes
processes emanating from the person of the therapist. Qualities
such as unconditional positive regard and steady attentiveness
are considered necessary conditions for therapeutic change.
These are powerful tools. The presence of positive regard designates the therapist as an important distributor of rewards, particularly for clients who have been unable to gain even minimal

acceptance in the world. Personal attention also possesses pow-er-laden implications as it compellingly suggests to clients that they must attend to themselves. In reviewing the intricacies of the client-centered approach, Barton (1974) considers the effects of constant attention:

> The client, then, is in the spotlight, directed by the total situation and the power of the therapist's steady attentiveness to be conscious of himself. This kind of attention to the client and waiting for his initiative in a steady planful way energizes the situation, is an enormously powerful living out of the belief in the organic self, and casts the client steadily back upon himself. (p. 186)

The primary form of intervention in client-centered therapy is the "client-centered response," a reply by the therapist which tries to capture the essence of a client's communication. This technique demonstrates a more subtle use of power than the more explicit psychoanalytic and behavioral strategies. As soon as the client-centered therapist begins with, "You really feel," the client is prone to the therapist's influence on several accounts. The client must focus on the self ("You") rather than on others or the therapist; on genuine experiencing ("really") rather than on fantasies or ideals; and on feelings ("feel") rather than on thoughts or actions. Eventually, as the dialog continues, the therapist unobtrusively replaces "You" with "I," a highly influential technique which urges the client to accept the therapist's restatement of the communication.

Therapist and theorist Eugene Gendlin, in a departure from the usual client-centered refutation of power, acknowledges about the client-centered response: "In such a response I attempt as plainly and as purely as possible to voice my impression of what the patient means and feels at this moment. Nothing else is as helpful and powerful as that sort of response" (Rogers et al., 1967, p. 399).

Additionally, client-centered therapists employ "reflection" rather than questioning as a means of exploration. The client is impelled to respond to an absence of normal discourse and therefore forced to focus on inner experiencing or on expectations of others' feelings. Also, the withholding of questions provides therapists with greater control over how much they reveal of themselves. Ironically, client-centered therapists can then decide "who is expected to reveal what about whom." Like their psychoanalytic counterparts, they are relatively immune from the scrutiny of the client and thus introduce an imbalance of power.

Behavioral Techniques

The central current running throughout most of the various behavioral therapies is an emphasis on environmental manipulation and control. The fundamental behavioral paradigm presents a therapist who is empowered to direct the flow of action through changing environmental circumstance, frequently in connection with suggesting a desired behavior. The therapist exercises power over the client's environment through purposeful arrangements of rewards and punishments (Prochaska, 1979). The principles of learning, which the behavior therapist relies upon to justify and augment his or her power, are applied toward such disparate concerns as violent acting out in psychiatric institutions and cigarette smoking in the general population.

Along with control of reinforcement contingencies, "suggestion" is commonly used to direct a client toward a designated choice or behavior. Given the power derived solely from the expert's status, a therapist's suggestions can take on great weight with the client. Thus, in techniques such as assertiveness training role-plays, a therapist is doubly powerful. While first proposing a course of action for a social situation (e.g., commenting to a rude line-breaker: "This is a line; please use it as such and return to the back of it"), the therapist will then secondarily reinforce the performance of this behavior as the client tries it out. If the therapist initially demonstrates the behavior, then yet additional power may be derived from the impact of this "modeling," a phenomenon to be more extensively discussed in the next chapter.

Individual techniques further illustrate the power embedded in the behavioral role. Included in the vast array of behavioral strategies are aversive conditioning, counterconditioning, and, more recently, behavioral-cognitive restructuring, to cite a few intervention strategies.

In aversive conditioning, a therapist accumulates power as a potentially threatening dispenser of punishments if a desired behavior or its avoidance is not enacted (Azrin et al., 1965). In counterconditioning, a therapist gains power by offering a competing response to a feared stimulus besides anxiety (Wolpe, 1971). Frequently associated with the treatment of depression, behaviorally-oriented cognitive interventions typically empower the therapist to direct and restructure behavior and thought initially through homework assignments (e.g., with depressive clients, employ list keeping and planning pleasure activities). Through these interventions, the therapist intends to upset and modify existing beliefs and behavior patterns through corrective suggestion. In this way, the cognitive-behavioral strategy also suggests that most behavioral techniques rely upon the guide/ teacher role to amass therapeutic power.

Psychotherapy Techniques: A Key Interface

The presence of the therapist as a highly significant and re-warding figure governs each of the therapeutic approaches. As an outgrowth of the culturally-ascribed power of nurturance, therapists disseminate such rewards as praise, recognition, approval, and affection.

Behavior therapists tend to be quite explicit about this phenomenon. Prochaska (1979), in discussing the place of social reinforcement, acknowledges its importance in behavior therapy but argues convincingly for its role in other therapeutic approaches.

Psychoanalytic psychotherapy clearly employs gratification and the withholding of gratification in order to influence the patient to change. As a transference figure, a therapist becomes a potential dispenser of love and comfort as well as a potential rival for these favors. Outside of the transference, the psychoanalytic psychotherapist also offers qualities like warmth and concern.

Walster et al. (1973) presents an interesting analog in the

experimental setting concerning the manipulation of gratification. The authors summarize a series of experiments designed to understand the "hard to get" phenomenon. They speculate that a woman confederate who is elusive, perhaps like a therapist in some theoretical schools, becomes more attractive to others because dissonance created by the participant's effort will then be reduced, and, secondly, the participant's drive toward the desired object will be increased by frustration. It seems then that the sought-after confederate, like the therapist in the clinical setting, gains greater social power.

We have already inferred that the client-centered therapist's relationship orientation is in itself reinforcing to the client. As Truax (1967) indicates, even Carl Rogers unconsciously shapes and influences patient perception through selective reinforcement. Such research followed in the tradition of the Greenspoon (1955) study, which first demonstrated that therapist verbal reinforcers profoundly influence the types of responses emitted by clients.

In summary, therapists of the various theoretical points of view all hold the power to reinforce and effect client expressions through purposeful techniques and unconscious cues. A therapist's regularity of attendance and consistency of attention are especially gratifying to those clients who have lacked such care. The opportunity to focus so intensively on the self is largely unparalleled outside of psychotherapy and is in itself a kind of psychological gratification. The therapist becomes an individual who can open the door to hidden aspects of the self; he or she is an interpreter of the client's dreams or a recorder of the client's everyday experiences. Finally, the therapist may offer warmth, concern, and even love. All of these possibilities provide therapists with tremendous leverage with their clients and empower therapists with greater confidence in their ability to effect the course of change.

THERAPIST BEHAVIORS

Therapists gain numerous privileges as a direct result of established therapist roles and intervention techniques. To provide some further appreciation for therapist power a brief outline of behaviors may be helpful. Far from a comprehensive list, the register that appears includes only those sanctions which follow naturally from the basic processes and techniques.

Psychoanalytic Powers

1. The power to confront the patient during any point of the free association process (particularly resistances).
2. The power to decide what requires clarification during the free association process (both transference and other resistances).
3. The power to allow or inhibit the unfolding of transference and resistances.
4. The power to determine what constitutes transference and resistances.
5. The power to choose what should be interpreted.
6. The power over style of interpretation (e.g., question, statement, etc.).
7. The power over the timing of interpretations.
8. The power to set the frequency of interpretations.
9. The power over the depth of interpretations.
10. The power to set a balance between interpretations and other types of intervention.

Client-Centered Power

1. The power to select what to attend to.
2. The power over the expression of unconditional positive regard and other therapist provisions, such as caring and empathy.
3. The power to choose reflections.
4. The power over style of reflection (e.g., deciding how closely to approximate the client's own words).
5. The power over how much to reflect.
6. The power over the frequency of reflections.
7. The power over the timing of reflections.
8. The power to form observations concerning which feelings are genuine.

9. The power to form observations concerning what is felt and distinguish that from what is thought or acted by the client.
10. The power to assess who is doing the feeling, either in the client's everyday life or in the therapeutic setting.

Behavioral Powers

1. The power to assess the environmental circumstances of the client.
2. The power to enact change in the environmental circumstances.
3. The power to choose what to reinforce or not, or what to punish or not.
4. The power to choose among a variety of behavioral interventions.
5. The power to decide upon the timing of interventions (e.g., setting reinforcement schedules).
6. The power to set the frequency of interventions (again, particularly important with regard to reinforcement).
7. The power to determine how broad an area of behavior is problematic.
8. The power to make suggestions and to request that the client try them.
9. The power to demonstrate or model desired behavior.
10. The power to define which thoughts are maladaptive (in cognitive-behavioral therapies).

The specific pathways by which these powers are expressed, as well as closer attention to the particular behaviors themselves, are included in the chapters on manifestations of power in psychotherapy.

INSTITUTIONAL POWER: AN OVERVIEW

Comparison of three apparently diverse approaches to psychotherapy indicates that each derives substantial power from designated roles and related interventions. In order to procure leverage with a client, the approaches all assume power to determine the nature and characteristics of therapeutic strategies. The three perspectives differ markedly in types of intervention and focus of intervention (e.g., insight vs. feeling vs. behavior). Despite the popularization of their visible differences, the triad share an underlying similarity as institutional sources of power: each seeks to furnish sufficient power for a therapist to have impact upon a client. This is perhaps a therapeutic universal.

Several other general speculations arise as we consider comparative approaches. Other approaches and techniques beside the traditional ones help to elaborate issues of power in psychotherapy.

(1) Therapeutic power may be greatest in intensity when some immediate and rapid change appears in the client, although such power may be less enduring.   In contrast to the "talk therapies" under examination (and to a lesser extent, action-oriented behavior therapies), the biological therapies tend to work toward immediate relief of difficulty. Pharmacological interventions, for example, through their own efficacy as well as placebo effects can produce rapid alterations in mood and behavior. As the patient begins to view this as a powerful means of intervention, both the perceived and felt power of the therapist rise in pronounced fashion.

As Abse and Ewing (1956) comment, these initial reactions to biological administrations sometimes give rise to a delusion of therapist omnipotence. When symptomatic relief wears off, however, power diminishes sharply and challenges to power by the client may ensue. Thus, the sense of therapeutic power wanes as the effects of the drug or other biological treatment weaken.

This suggests an important implication for verbal psychotherapy. Perhaps short-term, focused interventions (e.g., some behavioral techniques) engender transitory but heightened experiences of power, while longer-duration therapies (e.g., psychoanalysis) manifest fewer of these intense episodes but more enduring power.

(2) Theories of technique tend to differ to the extent that each relies on intervention vs. participation by the therapist as a source of power. The behavior therapies and psychoanalytic therapy emphasize their respective intervention strategies. Client-centered therapy, with its emphasis on the therapist qualities, leans toward a participatory orientation.

Yet the intervention and participation orientations are not mutually exclusive. Many psychoanalytic therapies are in practice relationship-focused, while many client-centered interactions are equally intervention-oriented. Approaches like gestalt therapy in theory propose a dual emphasis on intervention and participation and are designed to yield substantial therapeutic power.

In the gestalt theory of technique, some power is derived through intervention games like "reversals." A therapist directs a client to portray a role he or she feels is the antithesis of characteristic demeanor (e.g., instructions to hard-nosed person: "Be soft, be tender, try to receive from others"). At the same time, gestalt therapy is decidedly interactional. Concentrating on the "here and now," the therapist engages with the client and observes the inauthenticities or contradictions of the client. While gestalt power is similar to other powers in its techniques and observational characteristics, therapists intend to gain additional leverage through their active participation in the therapy process.

(3) Therapeutic power may be greatest during certain critical development periods. This may be easier to visualize if we consider child therapies, which typically take advantage of the "developmental power" of the therapist. Child therapies utilize a child's need for a developmental facilitator to establish a foothold with the child. Play is a basic intervention strategy. Play provides a medium for the therapist to develop a forum for communication with the child and thus increases the power of his or her change-focused comments. Not only is the therapist involved with the child, but puts into words what the child cannot and may have great impact with children.[2]

Techniques applied with college-age populations represent another example of power related to development. College-age young adults typically struggle with issues of separation-individuation. Several short-term or brief therapy approaches like the Mann Time-Limited Approach (Mann, 1973) utilize this phenomenon to gain therapeutic leverage. The Mann approach suggests a twelve-session, focused therapy and advocates directed interventions concerning the relationship between the participants. Such an approach naturally stimulates separation conflicts and allows a therapist to address these conflicts. According to Mann, the creation or re-emergence of the conflict in the current situation increases therapeutic power and enhances the opportunity for rapid development (Mann, 1973).

If the developmental period does affect certain kinds of therapeutic power, perhaps each of the three major approaches carries greatest power at individual points in the life cycle. Perhaps psychoanalytic therapy provides greatest power when a client is struggling with issues of extended commitment and involvement (i.e., perhaps ages twenty-five to thirty-five), while some of the behavior therapies enjoy the peak of their power with action-oriented populations like adolescents. In any case, it seems that a client's developmental stage may enhance therapeutic power if an approach addresses the developmental needs of the client.

(4) Lastly, individual approaches will probably be more powerful with some client types than others.   As with the relationship between action-oriented persons and behavior therapy, psychoanalytic therapy may find its greatest power with naturally self-examining individuals and client-centered therapy may have substantial impact with feeling-oriented persons. In fact, other less conventional therapies such as "cognitive-analytic" psychotherapy have been developed particularly to appeal to those clients whose personalities did not seem perfectly suitable for the standard therapy approaches (Raimy, 1975). A major factor in the therapeutic power of such approaches is their accommodation to selected groups of clients. Thus the issue of individual client preferences and contributions is particularly crucial with a volatile phenomenon like power and a changing context like psychotherapy.

Chapter 5

INTERPERSONAL SOURCES
The Power Within

Along with cultural and institutional sources, the personalities of the individual participants in psychotherapy contribute greatly to therapist power. Culturally-assigned and institutionally-assigned powers are ultimately filtered through the interpersonal bases of power, a domain which includes important personality and social status characteristics of both clients and therapists. Each therapy participant brings to psychotherapy unique personal qualities which touch the other and influence the nature of what develops between them.

CLIENT SOURCES OF POWER

Personality Sources

"Interpersonal dependency" is a most crucial client variable and one which enhances therapist power. Dependency sets the psychotherapeutic stage for power dynamics. Numerous theories describe dependency as concomitant with the illness state or with psychological difficulty (Goldin et al., 1972).

A good deal of research also supports this view of dependency. For example, William Snyder summarizes some of the earlier work in *Dependency in Psychotherapy* (1963) and systematically traces the generic role of dependency in the process of psychotherapy. Classical psychoanalysis sees dependency as endemic to patient status. In its more maladaptive forms, dependency is believed to derive from insufficient early gratification. Learning theorists also see dependency as pervasive in psychological problems and describe it as a conditioned response. In addition to the popular clinical perspective, the psychology of adult development suggests that dependency occurs throughout the stages of the life cycle and insures the necessity of the helping professions.

Given its intrinsic role in psychotherapy, how then is dependency related to therapist power? Perhaps most importantly, clients yearn for satisfaction of emotional and skill-learning needs in psychotherapy and turn to therapists to satisfy these needs. Hence, clients tend to assume a dependent stance. Client dependency requires that therapists have the power to supply sustenance or external direction (Parens & Saul, 1971). Therapists in turn arouse further client dependency by gratifying or partially gratifying these desires and raise client's expectations of therapist power. In successful therapies, clients eventually demonstrate more self-reliance and independence but usually not until they have adaptively passed through a period of dependency.

A brief survey of client types reveals diverse illustrations of client dependency. Sometimes dependency is a realistic response to the client's situation, while at other times it may reflect an unrealistic attribution of caretaking powers. In rare and extreme cases, as in symbiotic psychoses and some schizophrenias, a client depends on the very presence of the therapist for viability and provides the therapist with a kind of "life and death" power (Searles, 1958). Similarly, Adler and Buie (1979) emphasize that dependency is a central characteristic of clients diagnosed as suffering from the "borderline syndrome." They stress that borderline clients wish to escape from perceived helplessness through merging with a powerful therapist figure.

Dependency is by no means specific to extreme difficulties alone. A common form diagnosed in recent years, the need for self-esteem enhancement and recognition of specialness, represents a less pathological road to dependency. This type of dependency conflict is typically seen in individual clients described as "narcissistic" (Kernberg, 1965), but is by no means exclusive to such clients. Others characteristically engage in dependency battles and grant a therapist unwarranted power and then rapidly undo and negate this power. "Obsessive-compulsive" clients, for example, neurotically create a "therapist pedestal" and then chisel away at the therapist (Salzman, 1980). Finally, some clients may mask one form of dependency with another. For instance, a hysterical client might ask to be cared for in an infantile fashion as a defense against interest in adult sexuality.

In summary, regardless of the nature of the dependency and the power that is sought, nearly all clients present dependency issues. While some openly exhibit their dependency others vehemently resist it. Yet all seem to provide a therapist with a major source of interpersonal power.

Among other personality characteristics that lead to therapist power, idealization follows closely behind dependency in therapeutic importance. Gedo (1975) notes that clients tend to differ in terms of idealization and this tends to be an indication of their clinical state. Some express mild forms such as normal identification while others manifest forms like archaic grandiosity. The more entrenched forms of dependence, like grandiosity, will tend to impede any realistic relationship at all in psychotherapy.

While customarily associated with severe difficulties, grandiosity may appear in the omnipotent fantasies of even a reasonably well-functioning client for a period of time. Psychoanalyst Tilman Moser (1977) describes idealizing fantasies about his therapist:

> On the sly, my fantasies enlarged his house into a great manor or castle. I endowed his wife with truly divine qualities, and the metal of his automobile, when I happened to see it, became an object for furtive caresses. It was not just metal, it was meta-metal . . . (1977)

As Moser implies through hyperbole, a client can endow a therapist with power for a variety of reasons, many of which reflect back upon the person of the client. Moser convincingly goes on to argue that these projected, idealized qualities, while attributed to the therapist, are best understood as remnants of the client's own omnipotent wishes.

Demographic Sources

Along with client personality characteristics, background factors such as age, sex, economic status, and race affect the arrangement of power in psychotherapy. For example, Brink (1979) concentrates on the centrality of power issues in geriatric psychotherapy. He discusses a tendency among the elderly to see therapists as omnipotent and as protective parents with magical powers. Most interestingly, Brink concludes that successful therapy rests on the assumption of some of this proposed therapist power by the geriatric client. Among these other variables, the sex of the client serves as a common illustration of demographic sources of power.

There is emerging evidence that the sexes differ in their attitudes toward power. In a recent book on the relationship between power and love, Barbara Forisha (1982) argues that women deny their own power or refrain from assuming it. Fearful that their power may render others and themselves uncomfortable, women grow diffident concerning power. Men, on the other hand, find it difficult to relinquish power or to acknowledge its limitations. Clinically, it seems that female clients commonly place male therapists in exalted, even revered, positions. In contrast, it seems that male clients often diminish the power of therapists of either sex.

For both men and women, attributions of power based on sex are often as unrealistic as stereotypes outside of therapy. During a recent conversation concerning the practice of psychotherapy with the different sexes, a veteran therapist commented:

> I am constantly struck by the kind of power games men and women play in therapy . . . and especially by the almost magnificent sense of power or the total absence of power they may locate in me in their fantasies. I think that men are

more overt in creating a power struggle, as if secretly hid-
ing a desire for greater camaraderie and understanding.
Women, on the other hand, are more inclined to be compliant on the surface . . . I suppose due to socialization differences. . . . It is only later that their own desires for power
emerge. I believe it is only in the last few years that I have
learned not to play into these power tendencies, as I used to
out of my own anxiety, and to realize that underlying these
opposite appearances are some very similar fears and unacknowledged strengths.

In considering such power related to sex, it is important to note
that sex-related issues cut across diagnostic categories. In addition, they tend to interact with other variables like dependency
or idealization to form a constellation of power dynamics. In
relating several vignettes, Linder (1955) emphasizes the recur-
rence of sex-role related concerns in conjunction with struggles
over dependency and control, frequently creating a clinical picture that makes resolution of troubles difficult.

THERAPIST SOURCES OF POWER

Personality Sources

A critical therapist variable is power motivation. While there
are substantial individual differences in power motivation, we
might anticipate an overall trend toward high power motivation
among therapists. There is little direct research or assessment of
therapists' power motivation but several findings point in this
direction.

In its original conception, high power motivation is associated with access to having impact and the need to feel individual,
both of which seem consistent with an interest in psychotherapy.
In fact, in initial validation studies of power motivation, participants who expressed a career preference for therapist or a related occupation scored high on power motivation (Winter,
1973). Several contributions concerning psychotherapist personality characteristics support this finding. Both Henry (1977)

and Roe (1969) note the common empirical finding that therapists are characterized by a desire for power and this influences
their career choice.

The personal security versus personal vulnerability of a
therapist is a second important characteristic in regard to power
—a dimension in which therapists probably manifest qualitative
power differences. On one hand, "personal security" represents
a belief in one's own therapeutic potency and a tolerance for a
client's power. At the other extreme, "personal vulnerability" reflects a need to prove one's own power without a fully internalized sense of power. This vulnerability may precipitate intoler-
ance of client resistances, direct affirmations of authority, and
other obvious and subtle manifestations of power.

When discussed in the psychotherapy literature, vulnerability appears as a therapist's "narcissism" and in this context pro-
pels a therapist toward excessive power (see as early as Ferenczi,
1928). Ongoing therapy factors which influence therapist security and vulnerability include the following concerns: experience
level, opportunity for professional support (e.g., supervision),
number of current clients, the therapist's own current therapy,
publishing and professional progress, and stressful intercurrent
life events.

The security or vulnerability of a therapist is a most complex dimension to assess, not only for the outside observer but
for the individual therapist or for the clientele. It is clearly a
most difficult undertaking to acknowledge vulnerabilities and to
change for professional reasons; it is, however, a necessary task
for the psychotherapist. Moreover, it is not unlike the task of the
client, who is, after all, ordinarily charged by the therapeutic
process to examine him- or herself in such a manner.

Demographic Sources

Many of the same client background factors are also important therapist factors. Such personal traits as age, sex, and economic status frame a therapist's view of psychotherapy and influence approach to particular clients.

With regard to economic status, for instance, the vast majority of therapists are probably middle class (Wixen, 1973). Eco-

nomic status can well become a source of power with such therapists, particularly with low-income clients. Such a relationship is
not surprising. But financial differences in the reverse direction,
if even implicitly affecting a therapist, may also influence psychotherapy. For example, Burton Wixen (1973) documents several therapeutic traps in his book, *Children of the Rich*. Wixen emphasizes a tendency among middle and upper-middle class
therapists to exert authority inappropriately concerning fees
and procedures with wealthy clients. A co-worker of Wixen
finds himself assuming unwarranted power through the facade
of refining therapeutic procedures:

> You know, if I had it to do over, I would completely change
> my approach. Instead of seeing him [i.e., a wealthy teen-
> ager] four times a week, I would insist he come in five
> times. And instead of allowing him to take two-month vaca-
> tions to Europe every summer, I would insist he limit his va-
> cation to the two or three weeks I take. I was just too easy-
> going with him. (Wixen, 1973, p. 144)

Thus, there is strong speculation that a therapist's demographic background, in conjunction with the social status traits
of the client, tends to have pronounced effects on the practice of
psychotherapy. Along with pragmatic decisions, such as those
choices concerning payment and schedule, an entire host of
therapy-related interventions and guidelines may conceivably be
shaped by such individual characteristics.

Miscellaneous Sources

In addition to personality and background characteristics,
other personal and situational attributes may develop feelings of
power in the practicing psychotherapist. Among personal attributes, intellectual and empathetic capacities are prominent assets
for a client but essential qualities for a therapist.

Intelligence may be a particularly pervasive source of power
in insight-oriented therapies, where cognitive ability can lead to
more accurate and thorough interpretations. Empathy is re-
garded by many practicing therapists as the *sine qua non* for the

clinician. A number of theoretical perspectives, the client-centered and other counseling-oriented views in particular, have been quite outspoken on this point. Nonetheless, the role of empathy is still relatively underinvestigated and its relationship to therapeutic power largely unexamined. What may be particularly important in terms of power may be a therapist's perception of his or her empathetic abilities, as well as actual empathic skill.

RELATIONSHIP SOURCES OF POWER

Power also accrues as a result of the nature of the relationships, however informal and unexpressed, which are formed by the therapy dyad. These relationships reflect the interaction of individual client and therapist characteristics, i.e., their relational "fit" and shared relationship-based processes.

Relational Fit Sources

As implied in the Wixen example, an interaction of therapist and client characteristics sometimes produces great power and upsets the distribution of power. The interplay of characteristics can lead to a "therapeutic fit" of a particular level of therapist power.

Some combinations of personality qualities or matchings of demographic characteristics are perhaps more power-dispensing than others. While therapy relationships between male therapists and female clients are most common and perhaps among the most power-oriented, other pairs may reflect power concerns of no less therapeutic intensity. Both clinical concerns and some research support the importance of power as a critical dimension in the analysis of therapeutic fit (see Lieberman, 1978; see Friedman & Dies, 1974).[1]

Within the therapeutic interaction literature, a commonly discussed area of social status fit is the relationship between race of therapist and race of client. Jerome Sattler (1977) provides an interesting summary article on the complexities of power and race relations in psychotherapy. He maintains that race and feelings of "blackness" or "whiteness" create new interpersonal patterns or intensify and complicate existing ones. Between the black client and the white therapist, Sattler observes a typical paradigm which he labels "paternalism and the Great White Father Syndrome." In such a pattern, a white therapist assumes enormous power while the black client readily relinquishes it. In the most aggravated of instances a white therapist might discourage the black client from high achievement aspirations, "for his own good," infantilize the client about self-care and implicitly communicate that change happens only with servile dependency (1977).

Meanwhile, according to Sattler, clients may contribute a sense of apathy and powerlessness associated with their view of race relations. Thus, reinforcement of "Uncle Tom"-like activity ensues and clients feel impotent and excessively dependent (Jackson, 1973). In reviewing the now voluminous research on interracial dynamics, Sattler finds a consistent empirically-supported tendency for either white or black clients to be overly compliant in biracial therapy situations. Quality of communication is improved, however, when power issues are openly acknowledged and when legitimate professional power is clarified by both parties (Sattler, 1974; also Porter, 1974).

Whether personality or social status variables are considered, issues of relational fit have important implications for therapeutic work. Dynamics of power may be especially operative at the time of referral; certainly not all clients and therapists will form a therapeutically advisable and harmonious pair. When alternative therapists are available, individual therapists must be sensitive to compatibility concerns and be prepared to act therapeutically in the client's behalf. Naturally, as is so often true in clinical practice, self-knowledge about power by the therapist greatly improves clinical judgment.

Interpersonal Processes: Alliances, Modeling

In addition to the interaction of personality and demographic characteristics, a number of generic dyadic processes ordinarily enhance the power of a therapist. These process sources of power include therapeutic "alliance" effects and "modeling" effects.

Therapeutic "alliances," sometimes called "working alliances" or "therapeutic contracts," refer to the explicit or implicit relationships therapists and clients form concerning the nature of their tasks. Alliances sometimes include the personal qualities of the participants and sometimes encompass only instrumental concerns. In *The Technique and Practice of Psychoanalysis* (1967), Ralph Greenson describes the typical alliance in the oldest of psychotherapy approaches:

> The working alliance is the relatively non-neurotic, rational relationship between patient and analyst which makes it possible for the patient to work purposefully in the analytic situation. . . . The analyst contributes to the working alliance by his consistent emphasis on understanding and insight . . . and by his compassionate, empathic, straightforward and nonjudgmental attitudes. (p. 192)

Among others, Bordin (1974) suggests that alliances are integral to the process of psychotherapy and differ in detail but not in importance across therapeutic approaches. In other words, behavioral tasks contrast markedly from psychoanalytic tasks but both necessitate a contractual relationship between the participants concerning their respective tasks.

Alliances can generate therapeutic power by: (1) instituting therapeutic agreements which imply that the therapist is necessary for the ongoing therapeutic work; (2) suggesting that there are particular therapeutic tasks which are introduced by the therapist; (3) developing an emotional tie between the client and the therapist which increases the persuasiveness and attractiveness of the therapist (Friedman, 1969; Goldstein, Heller, & Sechrest, 1966); and (4) providing an opportunity for expression of therapist humanness which has the power to foster openness in the client.

Certain characteristics of alliances tend to effect a greater balance of power between client and therapist. The elements of therapeutic contracting and ground-rule setting, most explicitly enacted in the behavioral therapies and some short-term therapies, provide clients with substantive power (Mann, 1973). Here, the therapeutic power is subtle. Because of the very mutuality of the relationship the therapist's words carry weight with the client who is capable of sharing. In addition, alliances tend to be reality-based and present-focused and hence are less likely than other therapeutic processes to promote unrealistic expectations or visions of power. Thus, and this seems particularly critical, prevention of unwarranted power may be one of the primary therapeutic functions of an alliance.

Modeling represents a second relationship process along with alliances. Much therapeutic power is gained through therapist demonstration and resulting client imitation. A therapist may influence a client precisely because a client perceives the therapist as problem-free: a therapist becomes a role model for mastery of psychological problems. While there are other reasons for the therapeutic impact of modeling, probably few are as powerful as this.

A good deal of evidence substantiates the relationship power of modeling in psychotherapy. In a general overview of altruistic behaviors, Macauley and Berkowitz (1971) cite clear modeling effects in a variety of helping behaviors, particularly in therapeutic limit setting. In an example of a more focused study, Matarazzo (1968) finds that both duration of therapist speech and therapist silence produce similar patterns among clients. Jourard and Jaffee (1970) report similar findings with regard to therapist self-disclosure, a result which suggests that therapists' affective expression may facilitate similar client expression.

But perhaps modeling may not always maximize therapeutic power. Willis and Goethals (1973) report an experimental study in which modeling of helping behavior led to greater client resistance to therapeutic tasks and consequently a decrease in effective helping behavior. The authors speculate that modeling was not effective because the model was too forceful and the clients perceived important behavioral freedoms as threatened. Such results suggest that too apparent a model, such as a therapist who relies upon obvious interpretations or role-playing demonstrations, may actually reduce therapeutic power.[2]

The idea that some therapeutic strategies may be too forceful to be effective finds theoretical support in the "theory of psychological reactance." Brehm and Brehm (1981) argue that increasing influence pressure beyond a typical amount for a dyad will lead to increasing reactance and decreased positive influence. Thus, a client faced with an overbearing therapist model might well react against this in order to assert personal freedom.

Interpersonal Sources: In Conclusion

All three realms of power—the cultural, the institutional, and the interpersonal—prevail upon the course of therapeutic interaction. Of these contributors, interpersonal sources are by no means insignificant. We need only note that in accounts of successful therapies, clients consistently emphasize the interpersonal characteristics of the therapist rather than his or her specific interventions or techniques (Sloane, 1974). Undoubtedly, personality seems a primary contributor to the unfolding of power dynamics in psychotherapy.

III. MANIFESTATIONS OF POWER

MANIFESTATIONS OF POWER

The following chapters present numerous illustrations of the manifestations of power. Through analysis of psychotherapy structure, verbal process and nonverbal process, we catalog in these chapters the various means of power expression.

A significant issue for manifestations of power concerns the degree of power in a given expression. Power is exceedingly difficult to quantify, but if one wanted to, power would be an outcome of a therapist's potential impact with a given power manifestation, considering other contextual variables like client state and strength of the therapeutic relationship. Without a more precise means of assessment, the view inherent in these chapters is that the amount of power is highly variable, differing considerably across modes of expression and across many other client and therapist characteristics.

In light of the origins of power, we now turn to its manifestations. We begin with structural manifestations of power, which, although ordinarily tied to particular treatment approaches, are equally dependent upon the unique personalities of therapist and client.

Chapter 6

STRUCTURAL MANIFESTATIONS
The Symbols of Power

To identify manifestations of power as they arise in the course of psychotherapy, we begin with those expressions of power which pervade the structure of the psychotherapy situation. In order to review comprehensively these structural properties, we first examine power in the psychological setting (or atmosphere) and then explore its presence in the physical setting and in the pragmatics of setting (rules and procedures).

THE PSYCHOLOGICAL SETTING

Theoretical Considerations

Individual therapies and therapists differ in the climates they create for psychotherapy. By climate or "psychological setting," we mean the implicit atmospheric characteristics of the situation and its participants. These are characteristics like warmth or ambiguity (in either the situation or in the person of the therapist) which accompany and give life to the established techniques for change.

Psychological settings seem to vary quite a bit with regard to level of power expression. Nevertheless, one common characteristic stands out: the creation of the therapeutic setting is in itself an attempt at influence, as it dictates the atmosphere in which discourse must take place.

Another source of great variability among psychotherapies is the critical dimension of therapist awareness. Some therapists will be more conscious of the atmospheres they create than will their colleagues. When the psychological setting is part of a planned treatment package or technique, as is the case with client-centered therapy, a therapist will most often remain aware of its presence and, it would be hoped, its possible impact on the client. When the setting reflects the personal qualities of the therapist, however, an accurate appreciation for the setting may be more difficult. One generalization that perhaps all therapists would agree with concerns the mark of the sensitive therapist: he or she constantly attends to the moods of the participants and applies this to the therapeutic advantage and improvement of the client. Alger (1966), among other thoughtful writers, is insistent that therapists attune themselves to the issue of psychological atmosphere in psychotherapy.

Whether a psychological climate lends itself to useful or abusive power presents a complex issue. In many ways, the climate is not a static aspect of psychotherapy but one that changes as the course of therapy changes. Thus a climate of high activity may be therapeutic at one juncture and yet obstructive at another. It may be that the overall climate of a psychotherapy can only be assessed in comprehensive evaluation by the efficacy of the treatment at the therapy's conclusion. It should also be emphasized that with any given dimension of a climate, such as level of activity, an extremely careful appreciation for the treatment context is necessary accurately to assess its power implications.

Power can be expressed atmospherically in countless ways. For example, it may be communicated through the personal warmth and resulting influence of a therapist. But power may also be expressed through less apparent situational attributes, like ambiguity, a characteristic of the treatment situation which indicates the degree of clarity and definition of therapeutic tasks.

Several research studies, including the analog studies of Heller (1968) and Cohen (1959), demonstrate that ambiguity of situation tends to induce power-related interactions between interview participants. Heller (1968) adduces psychotherapy simulation evidence which indicates that reduced feedback to interview participants is facilitative of interviewee disclosure. The author contends that ambiguity influences personal openness, at least among those individuals who are primed for personal expression. In an earlier study, Cohen (1959) investigated situational structure and reactions to power and found that ambiguous situations induced more frequent power-oriented reactions and anxiety in participants. Thus, ambiguity seems to provide a fundamental example of a power-laden setting characteristic.

Ambiguity

The traditional psychoanalytic atmosphere is ironically colorful in its austerity, as it reflects a purposeful and unqualified situation of high ambiguity. The analytic scenario abounds in manifestations of power. On the nature of this therapeutic atmosphere, Leo Stone (1961) comments: "It is a tilted and uneven relationship in that the patient is expected to let himself feel and express all of his innermost emotions, impulses, and fantasies while the analyst remains a largely anonymous figure." We focus upon this well-known psychological setting for its illustrative expressions of high therapist power.

Ambiguity in the psychoanalytic treatment modality is embodied by the "blank screen," a therapist stance which keeps the therapist relatively anonymous and compels the patient to rely on his or her own projected expectancies. The application of the blank screen represents an expression of power precisely because it forces a patient to depend upon past history to cope with present interaction; it designates this discrepancy as the primary reason for psychological difficulty. The blank screen also ensures the effectiveness of a well-timed interpretation, since it summons a current re-experiencing of painful conflict. Collectively, the ambiguity of the setting along with the person of the therapist frustrates a patient from the gratifications of typical interaction, and eventually, from the gratifications related to unresolved neuroses.

The blank screen works in conjunction with "analytic si-lence," a professional reserve which allows conflictual concerns to surface. Silence is probably one of the most powerful struc-tural tools of the psychoanalytic psychotherapies. Silence en-sures that a patient confronts his or her own inner life, or so it is intended. But even more to the point, silence determines that the therapist has authority over self-disclosure—who reveals, how much is revealed, and what is revealed.

The power of silence is not merely the power to determine the content of discourse, but also the power to evoke and shape its affective quality. Silence is especially powerful as a stimulus for anger and fear. In Robert Lindner's collection of psycho-therapy vignettes, *The Fifty Minute Hour* (1955), an older woman client becomes fed up with her analyst's stoic posture and the coldness of the setting. Finally, she voices her frustration and protest:

> You're not human. You're a stone—a cold stone. You give nothing. You just sit there like a goddam block of wood while I tear my guts out! . . . . Look at you! I wish you could see yourself like I see you. You and your lousy objectivity! Objectivity, my eye! Are you a man or a machine? Don't you ever feel anything? Do you have blood or ice water in your veins? Answer me! Goddam you, answer me! (p. 129)

Lindner himself maintains the importance of therapeutic hu-manness and argues against absolute interpretation of the blank screen. He writes of his practice: "Neither the science of psycho-analysis nor the art of its practice depend upon extraordinary agencies. As a matter of fact, the only medium employed by the analyst is the most common instrument of all—his own human self . . ." (1955, p. 16)

Comparing the analytic atmosphere with other atmos-pheres reveals major differences. The typical climate in behav-ioral therapies is more open and direct and consequently less generative of therapist power. Client-centered therapies tend to present a more complex picture with regard to ambiguity. The therapist appears as a relatively unambiguous figure who re-sponds to the client as genuinely as possible. But the therapeutic task within this approach is highly ambiguous, given that nondirectiveness does not lay out for a client the nuances of the therapeutic situation. If a client chooses to struggle with the ambiguity, then by necessity he or she encounters the ambiguities of the self. If a client does not choose this path, however, then the psychological setting of client-centered therapy harbors less impact and the therapist less power. In summary, these established approaches offer diverging viewpoints concerning ambiguity and differ in their reliance on ambiguity to create therapist power.

The role of the psychological climate is perhaps best thought of as the essential meeting place of the technical and the personal in psychotherapy. The climate's significance for the therapeutic process clearly indicates that a therapist must be conversant with both the technical and the personal vicissitudes of therapy. In a thoughtful discussion of the contributions of the setting among diverse therapy approaches, Bordin (1968) concludes:

> This [the climate and its various aspects] means that a person cannot begin to be or function as a therapist without being wholly involved. . . . He must be sufficiently at home with himself to contribute to the humanness of personal encounter (as well as technical encounter) which is a vital part of psychotherapy. (p. 185)

The power of the psychological setting, then, is embodied as much in the "felt power" of another individual (i.e., the therapist) as it is in the power of his or her professional technique.

THE PHYSICAL SETTING

Theoretical Considerations

Along with the psychological climate of psychotherapy, the physical setting represents a standard medium for therapist expression in general and for the expression of power in particular. "Physical setting" refers to the arrangement and contents of the office space as well as the visible aspects of the person (therapist) and his or her accoutrements.

Characteristics of the setting often have important symbolic meanings for both client and therapist. In the eyes of the participants, characteristics of the setting typically express power, nurturance, or other salient phenomena related to therapeutic behavior.

Physical setting characteristics probably exert greatest influence early in psychotherapy, prior to the development of a deeper and more thoroughly articulated therapeutic relationship. Once power communications are finding more direct if not verbal avenues for expression, these background concerns tend to be less pervasive in the minds of the participants.

The physical setting in psychotherapy tends to intersperse power symbols with more unintentional and less influential setting aspects. Particularly in reference to personal items, distinguishing between attempts at power and less willful interest is rarely clear or facile.

A specific item, such as a suit jacket, may one day communicate as much with its somber brown color as a directed verbal statement; on the next day, clothing choice may have little to do with the ongoing therapy process. A few characteristics, like the arrangement of seating in the clinical office, ordinarily have strong and more easily discernible power implications because they are quite apparent and unmistakable. The seating arrangement tends to be more constant at the same time that it may also be more carefully considered by the therapist. All of these concerns contribute to the therapeutic power of the physical setting and to its "low profile-high impact" presence in therapy.

The Office Space

One of the most glaring manifestations of power in a therapist's office is the seating arrangement; one of the most power-laden of these is the psychoanalytic couch, which serves as a famous illustration.

The couch is an expression of power to the analytic patient in several ways. With a gentle persuasiveness, the presence of the couch may communicate that all of a patient's body, postur-

ing, and movements, or the lack of them, are open to the interpretations of the analyst. Similarly, the couch may serve as a
muscle relaxer or pain reliever, and thus become a manifestation of an analyst's love along with his or her power (Braatoy,
1954). In other words, it reflects unspoken support and inherent power to comfort.[1]

Yet, perhaps what is even more apparent is the relative positioning of the patient and the therapist. The "upper-lower" seating arrangement between vertical therapist and supine patient
conveys a hierarchical and uneven relationship. With the use of
the psychoanalytic couch, the patient falls under the doctor's ex-
amining influence and resembles the reclining infant dependent
on the mother's care. In fact, the couch may render the patient
more pliant to the therapist's suggestion or intimation (Stone,
1961). Other authors, less predisposed toward the couch, have
also observed that it may encourage a sedentary manner, passivity and atrophy as well as relaxation. These warring perspectives
exemplify the embittered controversy that continues to sur-
round discussion of the psychoanalytic couch.

In regard to the place of the couch in the setting, power is
further enhanced by therapists who position themselves behind
the patient and place themselves hidden from view. Haley
(1958), one of the most ardent critics of the couch, sardonically
offers: ". . . the analyst seats himself behind the couch where he
can watch the patient but the patient cannot watch him. This
gives the patient the sort of disconcerted feeling a person has
when sparring with an opponent while blindfolded." Images
foreign to psychotherapy aside (Haley seems to be talking about
the medieval duel or the thronely rights of kings), the analytic
couch tends to express an imbalance of power along with the
power to comfort. Most importantly, this is a paradox that commonly becomes a central element of many if not most analyses.

Other aspects of the office space besides seating arrangements may also constitute emblems if not trappings of power.
Collectively, these setting aspects convey a surprising degree of
therapist power. The general orderliness of the setting may convey a businesslike authority, a sense of helpless disarray, or some
intermediate state. The size of the space may suggest expansive
powers or a limited range of impacts (Cohen, 1952). Addition-

ally, the circumstances of the waiting area and restroom facilities can convey a "separate but equal" division similar to the racial statuses of the past.

Among specific office items, diplomas and licenses, or their absence, invoke the powers of knowledge and expertise or convey possible doubts about these powers. The presence of a desk and related paraphernalia may indicate the formality or informality of a therapist; moreover, they may serve as reminders of the therapist's life outside of therapy. This is most powerful with the client who desires a great deal of the therapist's attention. Finally, in therapies where specific objects or props are used, as in behavioral role-playing or in orthodox psychological testing, such ancillary items can also become extensions of the therapist's power.

The array of office manifestations of power are clearly quite numerous. Together, these setting characteristics set the stage in therapy for power cast as a leading protagonist. In his novel *The Manticore*,[2] author Robertson Davies (1972) captures some of the traditional features of a therapist's office. A young traveler seeks psychotherapy in Switzerland where he now resides following his father's death. He enters Jungian analysis with a Dr. von Haller and during one of the introductory sessions, takes notes of her office surroundings:

> This time we did not meet in the sitting room but in Dr. von Haller's study, which was rather dark and filled with books, and a few pieces of modern statuary that looked pretty good, though I could not examine them closely. Also, there was a piece of old stained glass suspended in the window, which was fine in itself, but displeased me because it seemed affected. Prominent on the desk was a signed photograph of Dr. Jung himself. Dr. von Haller did not sit behind the desk, but in a chair near my own; I knew this trick, because it is supposed to inspire confidence because it sets aside the natural barrier—the desk of the professional person. I had my eye on the doctor at this time, and did not mean to let her get away with anything. (p. 20)

A client's fascination with the seemingly idiosyncratic items goes far beyond the literary realm. While in other therapies the individual items will differ, their impact and symbolism may be no less pronounced than in Davies' account.

The Person

Of equal symbolic meaning are the articles of clothing and apparently minor personal items of the therapist. Decorum and style in personal dress are among the most obvious means of personal expression as they communicate a sense of power. For example, suits and ties may be harbingers of a businesslike desire for impact, while a white medical coat may dictate an aura of scientific and expert power.

Clothing can also express power in a more subtle fashion. Loose-fitting sweaters, like those worn by the fictitious character psychiatrists of movies and television, suggest an explicit informality and negation of power at first glance. However, these therapists manifest their power by their very frankness and informality. They may wear clothing that invites the client's trust and intimate that they (the therapists) need not depend on any uniform for personal power.

Along with dress, a plethora of other items typically represent or easily become manifestations of power within given circumstances. Pipe and cigar smoking are traditional vestiges of power as they associate a therapist with the founding fathers of psychotherapy and thus draw on the power of knowledge or expertise. Beards may assume similar meaning and may also have added power in their own right. Freedman (1969), in a study of interpersonal attraction, finds that beards tend to make men more appealing to women and increase their status among other men. Among other items, even as mundane an object as a wristwatch becomes an instrument of power when it signifies control over the end of a session, an incessant reminder of the temporal and limited quality of psychotherapy.

RULES OF THE SETTING

Theoretical Considerations

Other common manifestations of power in psychotherapy occur with the pragmatics of setting. Pragmatics refers to the concerns of time, place, and money that are built into any given psychotherapy. Decisions over when and where psychotherapy is to take place and decisions over its cost and related transactions—these are issues of which power is made and sometimes contested.

Therapeutic rules are by nature, by their prescriptive and proscriptive instructions, heavily infused with power. Psychotherapists who refrain from rule setting elect to bypass the assumption of such power, yet a certain tacit power may be gained by their open declaration of the absence of rules. Rules concerning schedules and fees can be particularly powerful because they tend to effect the client's life style. They may leave little of the client's life unaffected by the therapist.

While rules can be important to the foundation of a relationship, they can also be extremely abusive of power if applied insensitively or rigidly. A callous or inflexible therapist will find in rule-setting a convenient haven for aggressiveness and controlling inclinations. Clients can be quite vulnerable to misuses of rule-based power since most are relatively unfamiliar with typical psychotherapeutic procedures. It is thus the responsibility of the therapist to explain standard procedures; this explanatory function also supplements the already substantial opportunity for impact.

Rules become a therapeutic asset, and hence a helpful application of power, when they successfully manage the business of psychotherapy. They are beneficent tools when they contribute to limit-setting and defining, or provide a corrective experience with interpersonal agreements in contrast to the less satisfactory prior experiences of the client. For the client who has not learned to trust others in interpersonal exchange, a positive experience concerning the regulation and guidelines of the relationship, or an agreement to suspend such rules, may in itself carry great therapeutic weight and basis for change.

Time

The vast majority of therapies, regardless of duration, provide the therapist with extensive authority over the logistics of time and place of meeting.[3] With regard to therapy with children and adolescents, for example, Mann (1973) offers that the therapeutic power over time is substantial since it becomes associated with delayed biological and psychological gratification. In a phrase, the young client's developmental struggle is expressed in these poignant words: "When will I be big enough . . . ?"

Commonly, the therapist in most psychotherapies designates a domain of possible "open times" depending on his or her professional schedule. While not all therapists will suggest how often to meet, many will do so and most will set an upper limit (or minimum) on the number of weekly or monthly sessions. With regard to the individual sessions themselves, the therapist and not the client determines the length of a session, as well as the times of beginning and ending. This is as true of the more liberal psychotherapies as the more conservative and traditional.

The therapist announces these rules to the client and these rules become the reality of interpersonal exchange (Nelson, 1968). Usually a serene "It's time to conclude for today" makes the point, but the more controlling therapist may wear a wry smile when interrupting the client to assert: "We have to stop." Still others, perhaps uncomfortable with their desires for such power, while assuming the timekeeper function nevertheless append a time-related comment with a "See you next Tuesday." While attempting to minimize power at first glance, such a "friendly" therapist also expresses power by reminding the client who decides the day of meeting.

Place

The regulation of therapeutic contact, of what is allowed, and where, also comes under the auspices of therapist power. The usual meeting place is the office of the therapist. But whether the pair meet in a hospital, clinic, or private office, the client must ordinarily arrange to come to the convenient setting of the therapist. Therapeutic "house-calls" are virtually nonexistent and in many therapies interaction outside the clinical setting is forbidden and avoided.

Even in therapeutic approaches which present more relaxed rules, like some gestalt therapies and groups, the therapist appropriates the power to announce the acceptability of such contact. Moreover, therapists reserve for themselves the "loudest say" in the nature of sanctioned interruptions of the therapeutic process. Client vacations, client professional commitments, and other client personal obligations are often susceptible to therapist scrutiny and power. The psychoanalytic therapies in particular are notorious for leaving few client activities untouched by therapist interpretation.

Fees

The regulation of therapeutic fees presents an area of enormous power given the overall high cost of psychotherapy, yet the many therapists who offer negotiable fees set the field apart from other professions like law or medicine. Nonetheless, the client's emotional and sometimes inescapable need for psychotherapy allows therapists to exercise much power over fee setting.

Unmistakably, fees represent a whole complex and embroiled set of power and personal worth issues (Burton, 1975). From a therapist's perspective, fees may represent the quality of the clinical work rendered, the degree of personal appeal, or the hallmark of the therapist's status in the professional and civic communities. From a client's perspective, fees may be an incessant reminder of dependent status and of the sacrifice that must be made to get help (Haley, 1958).

Besides establishing the amount of the fee, a therapist frequently sets a deadline for payment and a guideline for frequency and mode of payment. The manner in which fees are handled may greatly influence therapeutic interaction. Haak (1957) observes that reluctance to collect fees can sometimes occur in order to inhibit a client's anger. Fee payment can reflect a variety of power manifestations, a convenient vehicle for both the therapist and client to communicate indirectly with each other concerning nearly any aspect of the therapy situation.

Payment for psychotherapy is unavoidably a sensitive and controversial area, one in which power is easily abused. Gelb (1972) suggests that therapists tend to misuse fee issues much as some families do, as a coercive symbol of rewards and punishments. Even the reputable therapist may on occasion allow fee concerns to influence the recommendations made to a client, or even the therapeutic work itself. All too common are masochistic clients who easily accept exorbitant fees and even derive pleasure in paying what they cannot afford.

On the other hand, a therapist who does not express a personal sense of power and worth by charging a reasonable fee serves as a poor role model to clients who have difficulty in seeking and satisfying their own needs. What this implies is that psychotherapy fees can express either too little or too much power, though either extreme becomes problematic for therapeutic progress.

CONCLUSION

The structure of psychotherapy, including its climatic aspects and its regulations, presents a most evocative area for symbolic communications of power. While presenting many diverse manifestations of power, these manifestations are often the backdrop for more overt and less predictable process expressions of power. Structure and process are both vital to psychotherapy and they seem to work hand-in-hand in terms of power. While keeping in mind these structural scenarios in psychotherapy, we now look to those experiences of power emerging in therapeutic dialogue and therapeutic action. Once the stage is set in therapy with the therapeutic scene, process manifestations of power assume center stage as the client presents his or her dilemma and the psychotherapy begins.

Chapter 7

VERBAL MANIFESTATIONS
The Power of the Spoken Word

There develops concomitantly with a structural framework a process of interaction that forms the core of psychotherapy. This is what is commonly known as therapy, therapeutic discourse, or, more colloquially, verbal exchange between client and therapist. Power represents a fundamental aspect of this interpersonal discourse. Expressions of power occur in a variety of forms including both verbal and nonverbal manifestations. With "The Power of the Spoken Word," we address the more overt illustrations—power which occurs in direct expression, power that arises indirectly as a part of technique, and power that accompanies verbal-related aspects of therapist speech.

DIRECT VERBAL MANIFESTATIONS

Theoretical Considerations

Explicit statements of therapeutic power, such as "I can help you with your problems," are infrequent in many traditional psychotherapies although they appear with greater frequency in some contemporary approaches (e.g., reality therapy, transactional analysis). The reasons for this relative infrequency are multidetermined. While the field's general consternation over power is probably a major contributor, of even greater significance is the nature of the psychotherapeutic endeavor.

Locating the source of a psychological problem is far from a simple matter and power-oriented guarantees of success are generally considered unwise in unqualified form. In an excellent contribution concerning "deterioration effects" or the possible adverse consequences of psychotherapy, Lambert, Bergin, and Collins (1977) summarize relevant research and note the susceptibility of explicit shaping and influencing techniques to exacerbation of client problems. It seems that such explicit shaping attempts may mobilize an individual's defenses and thus make change more difficult.[1] This idea is similar to the notion of reactance arousal, put forth earlier (Brehm & Brehm, 1976).

Despite such evidence as the Lambert et al. (1977) findings, there is also contrasting work that supports the appropriate application of direct therapeutic statements. Among others, Klein et al. (1969) find that direct praise of the treatment method by the therapist may be quite useful in some behavior therapies. In summarizing their work, the authors speculate on the critical effective ingredients: "The explicit positive and authoritarian manner in which the therapist approaches the patients seems destined, if not designed, to establish the therapist as a powerful figure and turns the patient's hope for success into concrete expectations" (p. 35).

By way of introduction, we can speculate that direct verbal expressions are capable of harnessing ill-advised power through unrealistic assertion of therapist prerogative. On the other hand, such direct proactive measures may develop confidence and rapport with a client and pave the way for actual change.[1]

Relationship and Intervention Types

Direct manifestations of power are either relationship-based or intervention-based. Relationship comments emphasize the centrality of the therapeutic relation or the person of the therapist in generating power for therapeutic change. Intervention efforts, the mainstay of a therapeutic package, stress the usefulness of specific therapeutic tools or cite past successes with a particular approach.

A colleague of mine describes the appropriate and helpful use of direct intervention-based statements, referring to the early stages of child therapy:

> During the evaluation or at the outset of parent guidance, I sometimes try to establish the effectiveness of play therapy with a doubting and ambivalent parent. For example, with the parent of a borderline child, I might explain that their little girl has a difficult problem with commitment to reality. I then offer that we have seen little girls with similar problems in the past and have been helpful to them with this therapeutic method.

With such an explanation, the therapist derives power from the confidence and optimism aroused in the parents. He or she works to persuade the parents to proceed with child therapy. Ultimately, the therapist hopes these parents will take an active role in the therapeutic process themselves.

Not all direct assertions of power, whether relationship-oriented or intervention-oriented, are quite so gentle and unobtrusive. When one considers the great variety of brands of therapy, therapeutic influence can sometimes become demonstrative and commanding. Particularly in psychiatric inpatient settings, where severely troubled patients try to maintain control over their lives, therapist expression and behavior become strikingly power-laden. The administration of drugs sometimes coincides with more forceful attempts to alter behavior. Physical restraining and shouting are far from uncommon, while self-injurious patients and unqualified manifestations of power are often abusive. Yet management of uncontrolled persons sometimes necessitates physical intervention. I am reminded of my first experiences in a private psychiatric hospital, where I worked during the summer following my sophomore year of college.

A recently admitted adolescent, believed to be suffering from manic-depressive illness, was causing quite a commotion.

Following an individual psychotherapy session within the confines of the hospital, he disrobed and ran wildly around the rooms of the small inpatient facility. Reaching the lounge downstairs, he selected a pool cue and proceeded to threaten other male residents while exposing his physique to several women patients. Attempts to intervene through calm discourse only seemed to exacerbate the situation. Much to my naive surprise, what proved most effective was an authoritarian command to desist along with a simultaneous disengagement of the adolescent from the pool cue. An even greater surprise was that I was the one voicing the ultimatum.

In light of such graphic demonstrations of therapist power, an additional caveat should be considered. Direct statements, as my relationship-based intervention in the previous example, may surface in psychotherapy as a result of a therapist's powerlessness, rather than a deeply felt sense of power. As with the adolescent in the psychiatric hospital, a client's controlling behaviors, however dramatic or mundane, may render a therapist's role futile and powerless. Thus a therapist may bluntly reaffirm therapeutic worth or therapeutic strength.

INDIRECT VERBAL MANIFESTATIONS

Theoretical Considerations

By far the most common expression of power in psychotherapy is not explicit but implicit in therapist verbalizations (Lennard & Bernstein, 1960). Few intervention or relationship statements offer a proclamation of power; most appear as carefully worded attempts to make impact upon the client. Often a therapist manifests power through articulation of the client's dilemma or consideration of alternative pathways of action. In such cases, expression by the therapist is indirect so as to avoid encroaching upon the client's sense of freedom.

Verbally implied power expressions can be particularly advantageous in moving a client from a position of intractable rigidity, e.g., when a client is reluctant to discuss the day's events. Indirect statements can be equally helpful when they serve to modulate therapist power, as when a therapist's direct statement presents too overwhelming a stance for a client.

In spite of such positive applications, the sometimes insidious nature of indirect power leads to abuses and efforts at manipulative control. An additional hazard with indirect statements transpires when the implicit power is openly denied by the therapist. The elements of therapist denial can leave the client helpless and without recourse. This is hardly good therapy and genuine, frank therapeutic discussion is virtually impossible under such circumstances.

To consider the relevance of indirect expressions for psychotherapy, Murray and Jacobson (1971) tested patient verbal productions and therapist verbal influence. The researchers' analyses of treatment tape recordings, collected during nondirective therapy sessions, revealed that therapist reactions could be reliably categorized as "approving" or "disapproving." Statements which were disapproved by the therapists fell markedly in occurrence following the second therapy hour, while client statements that met with approval by the therapist rose significantly.[2] The relative effects of approval and disapproval pointed to an attempt at indirect influence by the therapist—a finding which seems to support the notion that indirect verbal expressions are among the most powerful socializers during the psychotherapy process.

Relationship and Intervention Types

Most intervention-based statements fall under the rubric of indirect verbal manifestations. We have already discussed how such therapist contributions are built into the various theories of technique and represent sources of power to the therapist. Though part of a therapist's "pre-therapy strategy," intervention statements assume specific form during therapy sessions and become communications of power within the process. The content of interventions, as well as characteristics like timing, quietly embody attempts by the therapist to influence the client.

Examples of indirect intervention statements of power surface in nearly every therapy, suggesting that they may be necessary for psychotherapeutic change. Such statements are often recurrent and frequently amass great therapeutic power. An illustration from a well-known and controversial psychotherapy approach and therapist, the rational emotive therapy of Albert Ellis, is indicative of the power of these statements.

Therapist Ellis (1973) presents an initial session with a twenty-five-year-old single woman, a middle level executive suffering from constant depression, a sense of "unworthiness," and excessive drinking and overeating. In describing her troubles, the young woman offers that she is probably too concerned and wrapped up with herself. Ellis rapidly fires back the following intervention in response to her statement:

> No, I don't think that's the answer. It's, I believe, the opposite! You're really the least important thing to you. You are prepared to beat yourself over the head if I tell you that you're acting foolishly. If you were not a self-blamer, then you wouldn't care what I said. (p. 185)

Ellis' blunt offering expresses power in a number of ways, though he never addresses issues of power directly. First, he implies that he (the therapist) has answers to the problematic questions that plague and incapacitate the client. Secondly, he contributes an idea that counters the negative thinking or "wrong thinking" of the client, thus invoking the power to oversee such thoughts and suggest alternatives. Finally, Ellis substantiates his proposal with the power of evidence, a reference to the client's sensitivity to his previous response. While the flamboyant style and focus of intervention (i.e., faulty cognitions) may be specific to Ellis and his approach, the invocations of power threaded through the therapist statement reflect a more general psychotherapy phenomenon. Intervention-based statements manifest substantial therapist power and importune a client to react to such power.

Relationship-oriented statements can also convey power indirectly and arise commonly in some but not all psychotherapies. Selected therapeutic approaches, which see the person of the therapist as critical to the process of change, are more inclined to rely on relationship powers. Yet task-oriented or technical approaches are not entirely free of such statements.

Typically, indirect relationship statements influence the client to attend to the centrality of the therapeutic relationship and intimate that the therapeutic relationship is representative of interpersonal relations in general. In gestalt therapy, for example, a vexed therapist expresses his exasperation with a client by referring to their relationship and inferring that others may have similar experiences with clients (Kempler, 1973). Such a tactic enables the therapist to designate the current relationship as powerfully important and it permits a comment on the client's ongoing behavior. Perhaps the most forceful expression of power, however, is the therapist's implication that the client's difficulties are intimately tied to such behavior.

Educational Type

Educational statements, those references that instruct the client about the process of change, present an additional forum for the indirect verbal expression of power (and, now and then, for the direct communication of power as well). Occasionally, a therapist finds it helpful to explain to a client what is happening during the therapy process. Clients, on the other hand, sometimes find relief in understanding the process. With an explanatory phrase, a therapist manifests power through the ability to delineate an internal phenomena and give it some context.

The prevalence of educational statements varies across individual psychotherapies. Some therapists depend heavily on didactic intervention as a source of power. Others introduce educational statements only episodically or inadvertently. What does appear in many therapies is a therapist statement like: "You're having particular difficulty now," or "I know you are very worried about what you're going through right now."

In the brief psychotherapies, for example, part of the continuing education process of the client surrounds the choice of a "focus" for discussion, i.e., agreeing upon the problem area or concern (Malan, 1976). As one colleague inclined toward psychoanalytically-oriented brief therapy recently noted:

> Sometimes, just confirming that someone's idea of what's wrong really is the central concern, is what counts. Some-

times I say something that appears obvious to me, like "You have a difficulty in sustaining closeness with men" and I didn't expect much of a reaction. Then, my young female client rises up in her chair and nods in agreement. Clearly, we're onto something focal, and ordinarily, the client will continue from there.

I think that the process of finding a focus is a kind of learning process in working with someone else for both therapist and client. Sometimes the learning happens because of hard work and much thought; at other times it occurs through serendipity, but then again, it seems to me that learning is generally like that.

In such an approach, it is clear that the mutuality of the learning process is significant and perhaps carries greatest weight with the client. It is certainly vital for therapeutic power that a client perceive the process as mutual, vital for the vast array of intensive therapy approaches as well as for the brief therapy designs. Such expressions of power draw upon the knowledge and guiding powers of a therapist.

VERBAL-RELATED MANIFESTATIONS (PARALINGUISTIC EXPRESSIONS)

Theoretical Considerations

Along with verbal messages of power, the linguistic characteristics of these statements reflect the most subtle of power manifestations. Much speech-related activity occurs in psychotherapy without the awareness of either participant. This was discovered in the early studies of the anatomy of psychotherapy and continues to be true today (see Scheflen, 1973; Lennard & Bernstein, 1960). Throughout the course of therapy the qualities of language play an important role in therapeutic dialogue and meaning.

Paralinguistic expressions convey power when speech is used by the therapist to influence purposely the course of interaction. Characteristics of speech are important manifestations of power when they seem to support or disconfirm the content of therapist speech. Thus, the power of paralinguistic contributions is typically moderate but increases when they serve to enhance the power of more overt means of expression. Most therapists may be unaware of the way they are speaking at a given moment, but taped feedback can serve as a beneficial tool in sensitizing training and veteran therapists alike.

Uses and misuses of power are equally common in paralinguistic communications. A therapist can speak in a comforting, supportive manner and help relax the client, but a therapist can also evoke undue anxiety with a strident, insecure tone. What is perhaps most crucial is consistency in speech characteristics. Consistency is critical not only so that the client may come to trust the therapist, but also so that the client will experience the verbal manner of the therapist as consonant with treatment goals.

Power would seem to reside in several speech characteristics in particular: (1) language structure of therapist expressions; (2) tone and style of speech; and (3) duration and rate of speech.

Language Structure

The use of language to convey interpersonal meaning in psychotherapy is critically underemphasized in psychotherapy research, but therapists' language consistently encourages as well as inhibits client reaction.

Among expressions of power in language, the use of "Dr." for the therapist and "Mr." for the client is commonplace. In combination, these titles imply a sense of power[1] and establish guidelines for the therapeutic relationship. The application of titles indicates who has the power of knowledge and expertise and demarcates the relationship as independent from everyday relationships. The greatest power of the formal appellation may come with the message it conveys concerning intimacy and maintenance of a distant and advantaged standing.

In consideration of comparative approaches, such titles are no less evident in relationship-oriented therapies that frequently address intimacy issues. However, the manner in which a title or name is conveyed may be more significant than its appearance alone. While one therapist briefly notes titles and then invests the whole person in a cooperative relationship, another can remain informal and still seek the client's homage for the choice to do so.

Titles signify but one way in which therapist power is manifested through language. Language choice presents another relevant means of communication and a possible tool for influencing a client's affective state. Thouless (1978) distinguishes an affective function of language, as a means of arousing feelings, altering the intensity of behavior, and affecting attitude choice. In this regard, Spence (1977) says of psychoanalysis what might be said of psychotherapy in general:

> The psychoanalyst is not necessarily focally aware of [speech] as an opaque object of attention any more than is the athlete of his muscles' actions or the musician of his fingers' movements. Language is transparent; we hear through it to what is signified by it. (p. 413)

A few years earlier, Barton (1974) pointed out that once client-centered therapy left an extreme nondirective position, the therapist's use of feeling-toned words had the tendency to move the client to be more open about feelings.

Several clinical circumstances seem most indicative of the typical expression of power through language. Tubbs and Moss (1974) note that evaluative words have a way of communicating a good/bad distinction to a client along with the therapist's personal opinion. More specifically, marker words like "dark" or "terrible" tend to represent a therapist's reluctance to hear negative feelings related to a particular situation, e.g., medical illness (Spence, 1977). Unintentional influencing attempts by the therapist, such as reference to negative marker words, may well arise out of a therapist's underlying sense of powerlessness or desire to avoid a sensitive area.

Reliance on technical language serves to express power through a demonstration of the therapist's knowledge. For example, terms like "stress inoculation technique" or "directed imagery procedure" sound highly official and professional. Other psychotherapy parlance, especially if used repeatedly, conveys a negative connotation or redirects a client away from a topic. Phrases like "resistance," "defense," "games," or "avoidances" invariably imply a therapist's disapproval of client behavior. Such terminology frequently conveys a sense of power about what is adaptive for the client and about what the therapist will accept.

Style and Tone of Speech

A therapist's expressive demeanor, or style and tone of communication, provides another avenue for power. Tone and style refer to the way a therapist communicates to a client through vocal inflections and vocal mannerisms.

In a discussion of peripheral cues in psychotherapy, Sherman (1968) points out that tonal emphasis and related characteristics reveal therapist expectations and bear distinct impact for client responses.[2] Speech characteristics need not always correspond to other verbal or nonverbal manifestations of power. For example, Cain (1962) finds that although therapist speech shows no sign of disruption, therapists demonstrate avoidance rather than approach behavior following client oppositional responses (i.e., hostility).

Clinically, a range of therapist speech presentations is possible. On one extreme is an authoritarian manner. The therapist speaks with a rigidity and pointedness of tone, is forceful, thrusting, and strident. In every vocal quality, he or she communicates to the client: "You will have to accept what I have to offer to get well!" The therapist's power is expressed in absolute form.

On the other extreme is the tentative therapist. This corresponds to interventions that lack a ring of conviction; there is little force behind a statement and it may even sound like a hesitant question. The therapist meekly offers: "Won't you consider this, please?" In such a case, a therapist disavows or never assumes power as a result of a general discomfort with its exercise.

There is much room for variation amidst these diverse approaches and most of psychotherapy probably falls between the two. The most thoughtful therapist will allow for an expression of power while leaving space for the client's self-expression. Ideally, a therapist tries to communicate an air of conviction along with a sense of openness to the client's response and to reasonable doubt. He or she might speak in a clear, firm, and non-trembling voice and evidence comfort in speaking. The therapist conveys knowledge and expertise with forthrightness, but not with the penetrating uprightness of an authoritarian manner or with the quivering unwillingness of a tentative manner.

On the subject of therapist presentation, a colleague explains:

> With my voice and demeanor, I try to get across that I have a knowledge of the field, a sense of confidence about what we're talking about . . . yet I try to sound realistic about this and take into account what he [the client] is ready for.

As this therapist implies, when power is vocally expressed it needs to be modulated by subtle communication of the therapist's realistic limitations, no doubt a very difficult undertaking.

Rate and Duration of Speech

The speed and duration of speech, sometimes along with timing of speech, form an important cluster of process variables. In a prior chapter we noted that several studies have found a relationship between therapist and client speech production. Specifically, the therapist's pace and length of talking seems to result in an increase in client expression (Feldstein, 1972; Matarazzo, 1964; Jourard, 1970; among others).

In one of the most comprehensive studies of speech characteristics to date, Mehrabian and Williams (1969) draw a direct relationship between rapid speech and interpersonal influence. It seems that the effects of rapid speech are even more pronounced when they are accompanied by greater volume and careful intonation. Such research suggests that therapist speech characteristics convincingly affect the client's speech, though other evidence indicates that the influence may be bidirectional.

Perhaps any person engaged in a highly verbal enterprise like psychotherapy will occasionally take advantage of the power of speech. For example, therapists sometimes offer lengthy, drawn-out explanations of a particular behavior. The therapist might speak very softly and slowly, acting as if these words carry the "message of gods." He or she might continue speaking regardless of the attention, inattention, or forced attention of the audience. Moreover, the therapist might speak continuously and tolerate no interruptions, or deflect interruptions as the "client's reluctance to change." On this occasion, the therapist speaks as if he or she carries the floor and compels the client's acknowledgement.

Such a scenario infers several typical ways in which speech duration and rate can express therapist power. The therapist assumes unabashed control over the time and events of psychotherapy. By speaking slowly, therapists communicate that they can have impact upon the rate of progress of the therapy. By speaking interminably, they place their own words as the foremost contributor to the change process. Thus they use speech to convey that they and not the clients maintain power and importance in the psychotherapy relationship.

Certainly this is an extreme example. However, even with a less egregious use of speech duration and rate, it is alarming to imagine the implications for a client. It is particularly disconcerting when one considers the many clients who have never felt free to express themselves verbally, and whose self-defeating tendencies have recurrently led them to place themselves in secondary and subordinate roles.

Chapter 8

NONVERBAL MANIFESTATIONS
The Power to be Silent

Discussion of verbal manifestations of power suggests the equally important presence of nonverbal expressions in psychotherapy. In a current review article of nonverbal phenomena, Bahnson (1980) finds that nonverbal behavior may more faithfully and consistently express the visceral contents of therapeutic interaction than does verbal communication. Postures, gestures, head nods, facial cues, and less visible expressions all play significant roles in the transmission of power. We now entertain these various nonverbal communications of the therapist and address their clinical appearance and relevant research.

THERAPIST NONVERBAL LANGUAGE

Proxemics: Theoretical Considerations

Analysis of physical setting manifestations in Chapter 7 introduced the topic of proximity, an initial but enduring aspect of nonverbal communication. Important as a metaphor for power dynamics, seating proximity offers symbolic meaning concerning the limits of interpersonal distance.

The degree of expressed power indicated by proxemics is probably somewhat limited in and of itself. In some cases, the effects of physical distance will dissipate over the course of a therapy unless reinforced by other nonverbal cues. Yet such reinforcing communication on several channels is probably most often what happens. Proximal relationships go hand-in-hand with other nonverbal and verbal communications to enliven the therapeutic relationship.

Issues of physical distance can result in either wise or troublesome applications of power. A reasonable proximal arrangement may facilitate true interpersonal closeness in the client and yet provide an appreciation for necessary boundaries in certain relationships. A less thoughtful physical arrangement, however, readily becomes a domain for illegitimate power in psychotherapy. Some situations may seek to suit the personal needs of a therapist without regard for the sensitivities of the client.

Control of interpersonal proximity allows a therapist to shape the nature of the relationship and reminds both parties who has the strongest voice in the matter. Moreover, proximity influences the expression of client affect. In a colorful analysis of body politics, Fast (1980) describes how management of personal space can prevent a person from individual expression, especially when negative feelings are surfacing. He points out that actual touching (i.e., no spatial distance) usually inhibits a person from getting angry.

Proximity may also invoke additional power when it represents a discrepancy from the social norms of the culture. Arrangements like sitting back-to-back, as in counseling role-plays, portend to invest even greater power in the therapist and his or her technique than in external rules of decorum. But regardless of the seating arrangement, the gracious and simple comment, "Why don't you sit over there?" conveys the subtle or not so subtle message of therapist power.

Styles of Proxemics

Therapists sometimes sit distinctly close or distinctly far from their clients. Excessive proximity may prod clients toward greater intimacy and remind them that they are under the therapist's direct scrutiny. In fact, the client is then hard pressed to escape the interventions of the therapist. Of his psychoanalysis with the famous analyst Fairbairn, Harry Guntrip (1975) writes of their compact seating arrangement and its effect: "At times I thought he could reach over the desk and hit me on the head . . . . That this imposing situation at once had an unconscious transference meaning for me was clear . . ." (p. 146).

Excessive distance harbors its own power intentions. Sitting far from a client may imply a therapist's right to remain private or concealed, or it may communicate the limited boundaries of the therapist's investment, a telling message to any person seeking help and care.

With situations of high proximity, bidirectional influences between the participants may well occur. The nonverbal impact of the client on the therapist should not be underestimated, particularly with action-oriented or unusually dramatic clients.

Postures and General Body Movement: Theoretical Considerations

Bodily carriage and movement are highly visible couriers of power in psychotherapy just as they are in everyday life. Posture and movement impart unconscious messages which an individual wishes to keep from expression, whether a forbidden desire for omnipotence or an otherwise ineffable sense of powerlessness.

Deutsch (1951), in an article entitled *Thus Speaks the Body*, contends that posture is especially conducive to the expression of developmentally early and even preverbal emotional needs and fantasies. While Deutsch notes that postures need to be analyzed just like verbal content, he makes the further point that nonverbal postures communicate what is uncommunicable at the verbal level. Thus, in the psychoanalytic view, forbidden sexual and aggressive impulses might make their earliest appearances in psychotherapy through client and therapist postures (1951).

Speaking from the perspective of communications theory, another theoretical influence on our understanding of psychotherapy, Ruesch (1961) seems to agree with Deutsch's observations. Ruesch emphasizes that the operations of both therapist and client are frequently symbolic in nature. According to this communications theorist, as each participant eyes the other in action, their communicative aspects of movement will be telling and perhaps more enduring than any physical impact alone. For example, a therapist's open posture may work to compel the client to form inferences about the therapist's values and goals (1961).

Postures, as Ruesch implies, also accompany other body movements; many of the same power-related attributes are expressed with these movements. Among other contributions, Scheflen (1973) presents a film analysis of therapy sessions and discovers that the motoric responses of both participants are repetitive and reflective of consistent themes and feelings. Moos and Clemens (1967) report similar findings and steadfastly maintain that therapist movement is a critical determinant of therapeutic content and outcome.

While reviewing this growing literature on posture and movement in therapy, Bahnson (1980) offers the following general observation concerning the motoric impact of the psychotherapist: invariably, it seems, therapists will unconsciously lean forward when they expect important material from the client and this will ordinarily trigger a response from the client. According to Bahnson, this has been a subtle phenomenon in psychotherapy since its inception (1980).

Postures and other related movements are usually infused with power and are among the first signals of therapist behavior that a client may discern. The power of postures and movements is greatly enhanced by their tendency to indicate what is not being said by the therapist, or on the other hand, what the client may not be ready to receive directly. Nevertheless, these nonverbal communicators may appear concomitantly with related verbal material and work together to increase the base of therapeutic power.

Styles of Posture

Postures sometimes express power directly. A therapist may assume a position of power by sitting upright in an authoritative manner. Such a posture may coexist with verbal expression, say the regal interpretation prepared for the very moment, or it may even counter verbal expression. Such a therapist may enthrone himself in his chair in a bold manner, offer only a few soft words and still maintain power—the posture speaks more emphatically than words.

More often, postures express power indirectly through influencing the flow of a client's thoughts, feelings, and behavior. Significant cues about the relationship between the participants and about the therapist's inner experiencing include crossed or uncrossed legs, positioning of the head, and muscular stance. Postures often indicate a therapist's approval of a person, as in a therapist's friendly and open stance with a progressing client.

But postures may indicate disapproval and the power to express disapproval. Jacobs (1973) provides an excellent example of posturing from a therapy with a rigid, hard-driving man, a person whose resistances seemed unassailable:

> Then, one day, I observed the two of us: the patient as rigid as a coiled spring, his elbows protruding like iron pickets, and I, folded into myself, my arms wrapped across my chest, maintaining a grim and stubborn silence. I realized then what was happening. I had been drawn into an unremitting battle of wills. Out of sheer frustration I had locked horns with the patient, and my silence was, in great measure, a retaliation. Consciously, I told myself there was nothing to say, but, in fact, my body posture spoke for me: I was not going to say anything. (p. 83)

Clinically, these nonverbal manifestations occur much of the time in a given psychotherapy. Motoric manifestations of power are especially prominent at the beginning and closing of sessions, as well as whenever a therapist leaves his or her seat.

Consider the following examples of therapist behavior: placing one's feet on a desk to express dominance; walking with a confident gait to greet a client; springing out of the therapist's chair at a session's end to further emphasize power over time in psychotherapy; or purposely refraining from movement to demonstrate personal calmness and displaying this to the client. While it is likely that many such movements occur in all therapies, they may assume greatest significance in situations of sparse therapist reactions or talk-oriented therapies. In more action-oriented therapies like the behavioral therapies, these therapist motor activities will not contrast so greatly with pre-planned demonstrations or tasks.

Hand Gestures: Theoretical Considerations

Among nonverbal means of expression, hand gestures are among the most widely discussed in relation to psychotherapy and healing. The notion of power and hand gestures brings to mind the award-winning play by Mark Medoff, *Children of a Lesser God* (1980). The play poignantly depicts an intimate relationship between a hearing teacher and a deaf student. An important sign for the deaf student and one which communicates personal integrity is a thumbs-up gesture—an expression of "Deaf Power."

In other healing professions like psychotherapy, such demonstrative hand gestures can be equally graphic communicators of power and signs of personal impact. Bahnson (1980), in reporting the client-focused research on gestures in psychotherapy, emphasizes a tendency for clients to imitate therapist gestures and eventually own them. This suggests a power of modeling, a phenomenon which also consistently occurs among the characters in Medoff's play.

Hand gestures are primarily power-oriented at the same time they serve an explanatory function. They often occur when a therapeutic point is being attempted or some relational comment about the participants is being offered. Gestures may sometimes appear in a more casual form, such as the gesture of brushing back one's hair, but even such apparently innocuous mannerisms are only relatively free of power concerns.

Gesture Styles

Some gestures in the clinical setting convey power quite explicitly. Consider the therapist who makes a fist while striking home a clinical observation, as if indicating the necessity of asserting and standing up for one's self. Such an obvious action may have strong potential modeling effects, as the therapist sanctions the acquisition of power through this gesture.

Alternatively, consider a more delicate gesture. A therapist puts hands and fingertips together to form a crown, while sitting in an upright position. It is as if the therapist asserts the power of position and that it is here that knowledge resides. Such a gesture may be quite unnerving for a client, we might imagine, particularly one who is continually anxious and uncomfortable.

Other gestures represent indirect manifestations of power as they also indicate other feelings. For example, a male therapist plays with his tie. The act at first appears as only an expression of anxiety but perhaps more is communicated. The therapist may claim the power to offer "his goods," a power to be playful or a power to be oppositional to the therapeutic task. Moreover, by waving part of his uniform, the therapist coyly reminds the client who is the professional and who is the person in need. While symbolic meanings vary greatly and depend entirely on the situational context, power underpinnings are commonly present in gestures and shape the relationship between the participants.

Facial Cues: Theoretical Considerations

Therapist facial expressions may be the most influential indicators of power given that facial expressions are leading socializers in early parent/child relations (Tubbs & Moss, 1974). Research in social interaction and in psychotherapy suggests that facial cues provide accurate information about emotions and act as conversational regulators, managing the back and forth flow of conversation (Ekman & Friesen, 1977).

Krumboltz et al. (1967) find that counselors' nonverbal "attentiveness" (e.g., expression of interest, intensity of gaze) elicits information and facilitates initial rapport with clients. More recently, Lacrosse (1975) reports that therapists displaying obvious facial mannerisms (e.g., frequent smiling, head nodding) are rated by independent observers as more persuasive and attractive than therapists who do not show such expression.

Only an occasional facial cue does not express power or relate to power to some extent. Facial cues commonly embody a person's innermost feelings and thus can exert profound influence on the therapist as well as on the client. They have a great capacity to socialize and to direct the flow and rules for interpersonal discourse (Eckman & Friesen, 1977).

Types of Facial Cues

As an illustration of facial cues, eye contact is a vehicle of power in several respects. Eye contact expresses a territorial right to scrutinize or cast a glance where one wishes. It demonstrates attentiveness and thus heightens the meaning of spoken words. It compels clients to look steadily at themselves, as client-centered therapists suggest. Finally, eye contact either encourages the client to return eye contact or to look away, but above all to react to the therapist in some way.

Nonthreatening eye contact may be especially therapeutic for certain clients, as one New York psychoanalyst observes about depressed clients:

> Depression signals itself by, among other things, an avoidance of eye contact. To change them, I get my patients to attempt eye contact, small doses of it at first. . . . (Fast, 1980, p. 133)

Thus the therapist advocates the use of therapeutic power through nonverbal means. He employs eye contact to offset a sense of powerlessness or the avoidance of power.

Head nodding is another indirect facial manifestation and a convenient vehicle of power in the clinical setting. Head nods exhibit approval or disapproval and influence client behavior and self-concept. Head cues also increase the amount and type of response by a client, a finding replicated in several psychotherapy analog studies (e.g., Matarazzo, 1964). On the other hand, reflex nods may also diminish power by revealing a therapist's impressions when the intent is to withhold them. In many "talk therapies" a therapist may well reveal in nonverbal cues what is meant to be concealed in verbal expression.

THERAPIST LISTENING BEHAVIOR

Some power manifestations arise in the internal processing of the therapist and are intuitively sensed by the client. These listening or "noncommunication" behaviors (Langs, 1975) are frequently overlooked in keeping with the general neglect of therapist reactions. The neglect is most unfortunate because a therapist's inner life colors his or her interventions and therefore poses important power implications.

Within the nonverbal scanning and reacting of the therapist, power evolves as the therapist makes an assessment of the therapeutic situation. Power manifests itself internally as he or she sifts through content, relates to it, and tries to make sense of it. Such intrapersonal activity eventually gives way to the therapist's interpersonal presentation (Baranger & Baranger, 1964).

During the process of nonverbal scanning, two primary dimensions are: (1) style of listening and (2) focus of listening.

Style of Listening: Theoretical Considerations

The manner in which a therapist attends, although perhaps having no overt manifestation discernible to an outside observer, becomes recognizable to a client over the course of time. Hall (1969) characterizes various listening behaviors and emphasizes the powerful role they may have on the conduct of social interaction. Erickson (1980) echoes this general point of view while he investigates cultural listening differences and their impact on interracial interviews. If Erickson is correct about cultural differences, divergent listening behaviors may have especially troublesome consequences in situations of poor therapist-client fit.

Styles

A therapist may listen passively. He or she hears the client's outpourings and imposes little or no categorization or interpretative meaning on the expressions. Some therapists claim to work exclusively in this way.

Passive listening generates minimal power since the therapist makes only occasional attempts to influence. Passive listening sometimes expresses power if implemented episodically, as is the case with many therapies. The careful and timely use of this listening style permits a client freedom of self-expression without interruption and enhances the power of the therapeutic relationship. A therapist who is uncomfortable with such power, however, may lapse into a passive stance as a retreat from the reasonable use of power.

In contrast, a therapist may listen quite actively. This is largely what Theodore Reik intended with the phrase "listening with the third ear" (Reik, 1948). In active listening, a therapist attends selectively to what strikes him as significant and unusual. He looks for content that most precisely conveys the idiosyncratic personal meanings of the client, for communications that need to be highlighted and wrestled with. The range of such significant content is quite broad and varies tremendously across therapists; some therapists take into account their own internal meanings as much as those of the client.

Therapist imagery, daydreams, and other inner experiences all fall within the realm of active listening content, particularly as they annotate client communications and guide empathic responses (Kern, 1981; Whitman et al., 1969). Kern (1981) includes the visual screen images of the therapist during therapy among those internal phenomena that reveal therapist reactions. Whitman et al. (1969) suggest that therapist dreams occur more often than therapists report and that dreams provide insight about therapeutic interaction.[1]

Active listening clearly expresses therapist power. First, it authorizes the therapist to listen in conjunction with a prepared cognitive set. Secondly, it allows the therapist to impose some of his or her own reactions and associations on the unfolding script of the therapy. Perhaps most importantly, active listening circumscribes the interventions of a therapist, and in turn influences what a client expresses in and out of the therapeutic setting.

Focus of Listening: Theoretical Considerations

We have already begun to discuss selectivity in listening, but this area demands further and more careful attention. Nearly all of the major theoretical approaches define some dimension of experience that is necessary if not sufficient for the therapist's focus of attention. For example, the client-centered view emphasizes listening for "inner feelings" while the cognitive-behavioral view stresses listening for "maladaptive thoughts."

Designating the relative importance of domains of experience reflects consummate therapist power. The exercise of such power by a therapist is an application of the power of knowledge, a statement that defines what is critical and useful for change.

This domain of therapeutic involvement can afford a therapist unparalleled power. Through perfunctory treatment or neglect, a therapist can push to the side entire areas of psychological inquiry. Avoidances thus may represent a major opportunity for the subtle illegitimate use of power.

A therapist may not only inhibit a client's personal explorations but may actually exacerbate longstanding difficulties through neglect of anger, pain, or some other salient feeling. Yet, a therapist clearly cannot deal with everything that a client communicates. Some selectivity on the part of the therapist is necessary. Consequently, a focus represents a helpful means of organizing complex and perhaps even chaotic client difficulties.

Types

Therapists manifest power not only through a particular focus in listening but also through the absence of focused attention. Avoidances or "blind spots" represent a primary type of inattentiveness, as they indicate a therapist's neglect of certain troublesome topics (Langs, 1976; Racker, 1953).

Common sensitive motifs include any situations of great anxiety, aggressive confrontations, loss, helplessness, and sexual concerns. For example, a therapist who is disconcerted by aggression may tread lightly on a client's sadistic interests and concurrently direct the interaction to more neutral and intellectualized matters of therapeutic procedure. On the subject of avoidances, Racker (1955) maintains that therapist blind spots frequently represent an identification with the resistances of the client and insidiously interfere with the therapeutic process and the therapeutic relationship. He strongly believes that they are a function of the therapist's own fears and worries.

General states of indifference and therapist drowsiness are two other types of inattentiveness. A therapist sometimes evidences an unusual lack of interest following some intense affective expression by the client. The indifference can be a way of asserting or reasserting the power of the therapist role although it does so in a blatantly obstructive manner.

In an article entitled *Loving, Hating, and Indifference toward the Patient*, Greenson (1974) adds that indifference can be therapeutic in rare circumstances. He cites the example of indifference following emotional outburst by a psychotic client. Such a response by the therapist may communicate to a frightened client that the therapist will not be overwhelmed by the client's uncontrollable rage.

Drowsiness receives some limited literature attention as another adverse therapist influence. As a recurrent reaction, drowsiness is sometimes associated with responding to the utter helplessness of a client. There is some speculation that drowsiness reflects the therapist's own powerlessness, as it expresses that feeling and simultaneously re-establishes power through controlling the therapy (Dean, 1957).

McLaughlin (1975), in a discussion of "sleepy" therapists, notes that therapist drowsiness is particularly common with borderline clients. According to McLaughlin, several volatile clients have rendered him torn between rage and helplessness, and he has found himself retreating to drowsiness as a defense. He speculates that the unyielding demandingness of his borderline clients also had the effect of depleting his personal resources.

Avoidances, like other nonverbal and some verbal manifestations of power, can be remarkably subtle influences on the therapeutic process. They contribute to making the task of understanding power dynamics ever more difficult. Providing a label for these phenomena can, it would be hoped, increase therapist awareness of their prevalence in psychotherapy. As is so often the case with therapeutic practice, awareness of a process by the therapist is more than half the challenge in appreciating a client's inner world.

Conclusion: Manifestations of Power

The three chapters have been guided by the premise that little in psychotherapy is not power-oriented. The very nature of the process of therapy almost demands that power play an important if not essential role. Change, which is after all the central aim of psychotherapies, seems to require the impact of some new agent, whether that novel factor be professional intervention or self-initiated modification. The kind of change psychotherapy clients seek, however, seems to require more professionally directive intervention, otherwise clients could ameliorate their own situations. In a sense, we might say that power is basic to psychotherapy because consumers of therapy, its clients, seek the type of power to change that psychotherapy is meant to provide.

I have introduced in an earlier chapter the view in the literature concerning two kinds of power, one a more socialized experience and the other a more personalized, self-seeking experience. While this dichotomy is widely discussed in one form or another, it is difficult to know whether different forms of power actually exist or whether these forms are merely different applications of the same phenomenon. In other words, while the inner experience of power may be the same, therapists' choices concerning the application of power may not be.

With these preceding chapters, I have taken the view that power can equally be used for therapeutic as well as counter-therapeutic ends. This does not discount the possibility that different forms of power are at work. On the contrary, clinical manifestations of power often appear as if a variety of phenomena are at work. However, in the absence of any clear evidence or means for analysis, the discussion has concentrated on types of power based on the context of the situation and the therapist's application. Further discussion is left for the chapter on uses and misuses of power which follows.

Chapter 9

USES AND MISUSES
The Reigns of Power

Theoretical analyses of power as well as of its sources and manifestations lead to a veritable landscape of implications for clinical practice. To provide some sense of these implications, Chapter 9 presents a brief discourse on the most common clinical advantages and liabilities of power. This abridged discussion of clinical practice indications underlines the premise that power is a valuable as well as sometimes perilous enterprise, a point further refined by the uses and abuses themselves.

THE USES OF POWER

Among many therapeutic uses of power, the following are among the most prevalent and the most vital for the therapeutic process. Power can be used by the psychotherapist in a variety of ways:

As an impetus for interventions

Prompted by therapeutic technique or by the person of the therapist, the feeling of power abets a therapist in moving toward therapeutic action and in initiating discourse. To offer a convincing and worthwhile intervention, a therapist must believe in his or her ability to have meaningful impact.[1] Without confidence in his or her own power, efforts with the client will be largely inconsequential.

Power as a leverage for intervention may be especially important to high dissonance therapies (e.g., some cognitive-behavioral approaches, some psychoanalytic therapies) in which a therapist is expected frequently to interrupt or confront a client's maladaptive approach. Some therapeutic approaches rely heavily on demonstrative displays of power as a kind of impetus for therapist intervention. In a "paradoxical injunction," for example, a therapy strategy employed in some individual and family therapies and named by therapist Jay Haley, the clinician purposely attempts to get a client to perform a neurotic task. Once this unusual goal is achieved, either the client's healthy resistance will be aroused or the therapist will gain some control over the client's maladaptive behavior. In either case, Haley contends, a pathway to change is created (Brehm, 1976).

While such an approach tends to be controversial, it also receives some empirical support from social psychological research on propaganda. Cohen, Terry, and Jones (1959) find in their propaganda study that subjects can be mobilized in a desired direction through the implementation of forced choice scenarios like the paradoxical situation in psychotherapy. Despite research support, the long-range psychotherapeutic implications of such manipulations are unclear and potentially destructive to the client. On the whole, the effects of power techniques in psychotherapy must always be considered along with the longitudinal impact for clients.

To enhance the therapeutic relationship

In contrast to this first use, which implies that power is a kind of fuel for therapist interventions, a second function for power involves its more nonspecific effects. Within the psychotherapeutic relationship, a therapist's power introduces a key dimension with which the client wrestles or engages. Since power is ordinarily valued, the therapist's power tends to increase his or her appeal as well as the appeal of a potential relationship between the two (i.e., to the client).

Power in the relationship in psychotherapy is utilized by several theoretical schools. Gestalt therapy, for example, is an approach which relies quite heavily on the magnetism of personal power in the therapeutic relationship. Gestalt therapists tend to invite the client to engage directly and deeply with the therapist. Friedman (1969), in an article based on the psychoanalytic approach to psychotherapy, stresses a necessary and useful persuasiveness of the analyst based on a strong emotional tie with the client. In discussion of the therapeutic alliance between analyst and analysand, Friedman contends that power must influence the relationship in order to compete against the strength of the client's primitive drives.

Whatever the therapist's theoretical orientation, one point concerning power and the therapeutic relationship stands clear. Power can be misused relationally in any brand of psychotherapy, particularly as it rigidly dictates the nature of a relationship with the client.

As an identificatory figure for the client

A therapist communicates a way of being in the world. As the therapist demonstrates a capacity for personal impact, the invested client is likely to pick up some sense of this power over time. The process of identification is not necessarily a conscious one for either party, though it nonetheless poses important therapeutic consequences for a client previously deprived of any real power. While countermodeling effects sometimes occur and a client reacts against the therapist's example, these oppositional effects are probably less frequent than standard identification.

Even when identification with therapist power occurs, it may remain important for clients to believe their behavior is their own choice (Frankl, 1965; May, 1972). Evidence from social psychology implies that clients will tend to experience obvious therapist modeling attempts as threats to freedom and these clients will resist the therapist's efforts (Willis & Goethals, 1973).

Identification is a phenomenon that traverses the different perspectives on psychotherapy. In a study of comparative approaches, Birk and Brinkley (1969) maintain that identification with the therapist is as pervasive in the behavior therapies as in psychoanalysis, as each strategy attempts to promote its own treatment goals.

As an assessment tool

Therapist power feelings also serve as a means of assessing the nature of the client's personality. Affective reactions of a therapist, when they represent a response to client-assigned therapist roles, reveal important and concealed information about client needs and fantasies.

Therapist power reactions are particularly requisite as an evaluation tool when little other client information is available (e.g., with a taciturn or withdrawn client). The experience of unusually high power may strike a therapist as quite foreign to his or her own personality, for example, yet point toward a client who embellishes others with unrealistic and inordinate power. The therapist then either shares this information with the client, or reserves it for future application.

Harms (1960) is a proponent of the use of informative therapist feelings as a clue to the reactions of the client. In regard to more specific therapeutic uses, Tauber (1954) advocates the use of therapist feelings as: (1) a means of understanding the level or intensity of therapeutic contact; (2) a sign of resistance; or (3) an indicator of areas of client strength and as a basis for hopefulness.

As a sign of interaction issues

In intensive psychotherapy, therapist reactions can collectively provide a barometer of the state of therapeutic interaction.[2] Like other reactions, power responses are helpful as information sources in several ways.

First, therapist power feelings indicate the relative positioning of the dyad with regard to power at any given time. They may also reveal hidden tensions, as well as suggest the countertherapeutic direction of a particular interaction pattern. Secondly, therapist power feelings sometimes mirror client feelings whether the client expresses these feelings or not. This appears to be a common but underinvestigated interpersonal phenomenon in psychotherapy.

In regard to this use of power, the psychology of attributions postulates: inferences made about other persons contain the unique element that one can infer another's feelings from one's own feelings (DeCharms, 1968). Langs (1976), writing in the psychoanalytic context, concurs with this point of view and adds several interactional uses, including how a client influences therapist communication and which of the participants exerts the greatest influence. Gelb (1972) also writes from the psychoanalytic orientation and speaks even more forcefully concerning the importance of these interaction issues and their understanding. If therapist power feelings can be correctly appreciated in relation to a client's life, Gelb argues, then a real redistribution of his or her power in the world at large is tenable.

To sensitize the therapist to the limits of power and to their open acknowledgement

Awareness of the experience of power inevitably compels therapists to confront the limitations of their power. If they are sincere with themselves or successfully partake of professional consultation, therapists may apply their awareness of power toward detecting and understanding therapeutic errors. Undoubtedly, misuses of power and therapeutic errors share a close relationship that may at times be quite obstructive to the therapy process.

A number of authors have contributed on the topic of therapist limitations and therapist expression, both in terms of power and in regard to therapist reactions in general. In summarizing research concerning the place of therapist reactions in effective psychotherapy, Singer and Luborsky (1977) conclude:

> Therapists who have less anxiety and less conflict about their own feelings are not as personally affected by the patient's expression of emotions. . . . They [the therapists] are able to deal with their patients much more therapeutically, allowing the patients to explore their feelings. (p. 112)

The comments of Singer and Luborsky may be particularly appropriate for certain treatment strategies, such as the client-centered approach. On this note, Barton (1974) observes reflectively that as the client-centered school moved away from its original nondirective approach, it sanctioned therapists to apply expressivity and intuition more freely, which included an acknowledgement of confusion and limitations. What is now considered vital, Barton seems to suggest, is that a therapist's level of expression must be consonant with the client's level.[3]

Concerning therapist expression in therapeutic discourse, Schulman et al. (1964) discuss the ameliorative implications of a more open therapist demeanor. Besides increasing the therapist's awareness of limitations and bringing these into more honest dialogue, therapist expression may help clients to become increasingly comfortable with their own difficult feelings and their own limitations. This is particularly true in regard to inner experiences like shame and doubt which are not often acceptable in public interaction.

In general, while some writers have nicely articulated the role of therapist expression of power and the limits of power, it is clearly difficult to state in anything approaching a categorical manner when the open expression of such feelings should occur.

To foster confidence and hope

Therapists introduce many complex personal elements into the therapeutic equation and power is easily one of the most vital. Power instills in therapists a conviction that they are "up to the therapeutic task." They begin to believe they can offer help and expertise in their own unique way. Power can also persuade clients that, even in the midst of their despair, they can be helped. For both participants, power is a primary reason for hope in the psychotherapeutic process and in the relationship that develops between them.

The place of hope in psychotherapy, emphasized in most compelling fashion by Jerome Frank but also by other knowledgeable practitioners (see Rosenthal & Frank, 1956), cannot be overemphasized. The role of power in the creation and continuation of hope is perhaps no less essential. Recently, in *Freud and the Soul* (1982), Bruno Bettelheim eloquently suggested that the power of a therapist's "essential humanness" is a prerequisite for eventual hope and change.

The Misuses of Power

As a way of inducing client powerlessness

In one of the most unfortunate applications of power, therapists may flex their own power as a way of proving how powerless and dependent the client really is. Through sharp contrast, such a therapist compels the client to concede to a subordinate position, the very status the therapist strives to avoid.[4] For example, a therapist presents him- or herself as the "epitome of health" and leaves the client feeling sickly and helpless in comparison with such a lofty image. Such power is power laced with aggression as it seeks to move the client away from interaction with the therapist.

The forced induction of client powerlessness may indeed grow from the therapist's own sense of futility. Bieber (1972), in an interesting piece entitled *Sex and Power*, addresses the fusion of power and sexuality in psychotherapy and suggests that sexual reinforcement is sometimes used as a leverage for power by the practitioner. Bieber maintains that sadistic inclinations which emerge in therapy, either from the person of the therapist or the person of the client, stem from an underlying sense of sexual powerlessness. According to Bieber, sadism in therapy can then be understood as the illusion of power through the pain or suffering of others.[5]

There is compelling empirical support for the notion that powerlessness results in the attempt to secure the power of others. Goodstadt and Hjelle (1974), for example, report several laboratory studies in which individuals who perceive themselves as powerless tend to invoke coercive means of persuasion against others deemed more powerful.

Avoiding the experience of power

There are many reasons for the avoidance of power on both the professional and the individual levels, many of which are noted in Chapter 2. For certain, power is something of a taboo topic in the field of psychotherapy and the clinical practitioner sometimes neglects its role in the therapy process. Avoidance on an individual level is in itself a misuse of power since it breeds fallacies concerning clinical interaction. When power is denied, important communications of both client and therapist are lost or not discussed. This is a tremendous professional disservice to the client. The neglect of power is a misuse inherent in a number of treatment strategies but one that nonetheless can be offset by the sensitive practice of individual psychotherapists.

As early as 1941, Otto Fenichel, one of the leading psychoanalysts of the era, cautioned against the denial of troublesome feelings. He seemed to imply that such defensiveness would be a suppression of the human freedom of the therapist. Barchilon (1958), writing some years later, attacked the then fledgling counseling strategies for their avoidance of power. According to Barchilon, the avoidant counseling therapist reflects: "If I do not say anything, I cannot possibly hurt them" (1958). Clearly, he felt that this passivity was hardly appropriate for the practice of psychotherapy or counseling.

On the likely consequences of avoidance, Gadpaille (1972) stringently adheres to the view that neglect of power may lead to endless stalemate and eventual failure in psychotherapy. In a contemporary illustration of the dilemma that Gadpaille speaks about, Harris (1982) contributes a brief piece on introductory attempts at "feminist psychotherapy," a therapy developed to address women's difficulties as a result of social forces.

Harris observes a tendency among feminist therapists to decline or reject the assumption of therapeutic power, or any power related to expert and professional status. She speculates that for these therapists, power is still too closely associated with authoritarianism and rigid sex-role ideologies and thus little change occurs in their therapies. It may be necessary for a new outlook concerning power to emerge, Harris seems to intimate, in order for this political brand of psychotherapy to become truly effective (1982).

As a case of therapist emotional withdrawal

Power is often manifested in therapists' reluctance to delve into certain key areas or in their emotional withdrawal from the client. A pervasive problem throughout many psychotherapies, withdrawal assumes its most glaring and obstructive forms in the premature termination of psychotherapy. In premature termination, therapists literally disengage as a way of exerting power when they feel in danger of losing power (Hiatt, 1978).

With regard to therapist patterns overall, Cutler (1958) shows that therapist interventions are more likely defensively-oriented than task-oriented when the patient's behavior is conflict-laden for the therapist. Berman (1949), in discussing the client's reactions to such withdrawals, makes the now widely acknowledged observation that many intuitive clients know when a therapist is reacting. Clients tend to be aware of the therapist's defensive tendencies and adjust their behavior accordingly.

This form of abuse of power has numerous ramifications beside premature termination, including therapeutic impasses and distorted therapist reports. There is an unequivocal need for closer examination of therapist withdrawal as a flagrant misuse of power.

Obscuring empathy and understanding

As with other therapist feelings, power in extreme forms interferes with necessary sensory and intellective functions. When misused, power predominates over the therapist's acquisition and appreciation of the client's communications in light of the client's past or present circumstances. Moreover, therapists unduly absorbed in their own power or the power of their technique can become insensitive and detached from the felt powerlessness of their clients. Yet therapists who negate their own power experiences may be able to relate to a client's futility but not to the client's increasing sense of impact with improvement.

While some authors contend that any therapist reaction obscures empathy and understanding (Reich, 1951), a more reasonable view suggests that excessive, unrealistic, or purely self-originating feelings present therapeutic difficulties. Baum (1973) comments that empathy is endangered when the stress of the therapist's own intense emotions, whatever their content, colors his or her grasp of the therapeutic situation.

As a typical but countertherapeutic response to the client

Many clients, entrenched in longstanding patterns of living, may elicit responses from therapists that resemble the responses of the client's friends or relatives. If these responses stand unrecognized by the therapist, the dyad continues to replay self-defeating or neurotic patterns of power interactions. If recognized, the therapist's response may offer insight into enduring client dynamics. Certain approaches, like the gestalt and psychoanalytic, even rely on this phenomenon as part of their treatment strategies.

Recurrent but ill-advised therapist responses can lay the groundwork for what Langs (1976) termed "interactional resistances." These resistances refer to episodes of shared defensiveness and avoidance in the therapeutic field; psychotherapy may even become an incessant pattern of manipulative power reactions. Aaron (1974) adds that problematic, current life events can render a therapist vulnerable to such mutually defeating patterns of discourse, particularly as the therapist's illness or injury contributes to feelings of powerlessness.

As an example of such an interactional pattern, consider a young female client who bestows all the imagined trappings of power onto her older male therapist. Failing to acknowledge the unrealistic quality of her expectations and concern about his age, the therapist adopts an inordinately powerful father role. The pattern continues indefinitely and actually supports and exacerbates the client's conviction that older men are indeed so powerful. In the final analysis, confusion prevails over both parties as little therapeutic progress ensues. Perhaps the therapist may even join the client in a shared sense of powerlessness concerning the fate of the therapy. Even worse, he may protect his revered position by attributing the impasse solely to the motivations of the client.

For the purpose of self-aggrandizement

Power which intends to bolster the image of the therapist is perhaps the most infamous of therapy abuses. Whether technique- or relationship-directed, power symbolizes the prowess of the therapist on the plane of psychotherapy.

Therapist self-aggrandizement represents an inappropriate desire for the client to satisfy therapist needs for power and esteem not met elsewhere. Frequently, aggrandizement through power occurs in a therapist's fantasies during or after a therapy session. Eventually, it finds its way into the setting through nonverbal communication or the more subtle expressions accompanying the explanation of psychotherapy guidelines.

Searles (1966) insightfully points out that the therapist's search for a sense of omnipotence, with all its irrational underpinnings, is often the motivation behind self-aggrandizement. In a similar light, Murphy (1973) and Kernberg (1965) both find that self-aggrandizement frequently manifests itself in psychotherapy as an unusual and unreasonable certainty concerning therapeutic outcome. While hopefulness and confidence may be important for successful therapy, the authors seem to imply, an unwarranted view of one's abilities is not.

Imposition of values

Discussion of the guide role in psychotherapy suggested the possible overlap between psychotherapy and moral values. Sometimes, an individual therapist may find in psychotherapy a convenient podium from which to preach a set of values or a view of the world. Such assumed power becomes interspersed with a particular theoretical point of view and presents an imposing dogma to the client. The therapist's words may have great weight with the client, particularly when helpful interventions accompany more proselytizing efforts.

The potential significance of the therapist's words has long been a source of grave concern. Among many others, Freud speaks vehemently in opposition to therapist evangelism; he warned that active efforts to teach or proselytize will have detrimental effects and will likely repeat the mistakes of childhood (Langs, 1976).[6]

In an interesting contemporary article, Wile (1972) makes the cogent argument that a modern form of value indoctrination is "regression to orthodoxy." A most insidious form of coercion, this phenomenon refers to a therapist's retreat to the strict tenets of theoretical perspective for self-protective reasons and to the forced application of those tenets in therapy. Wile seems to suggest that regression to orthodoxy is more prevalent in difficult sessions than many therapists will readily acknowledge.

In spite of the best intentions, nearly all therapists will occasionally convey personal values to their clients. This would seem to be a natural outgrowth of working together, perhaps for an extensive period of time, on matters close to the heart of a person. The apparent reality of such communications in psychotherapy necessitates that therapists remain alert to their occurrence.

The many guises of power make therapist circumspection and awareness essential. The therapist must be equally cognizant of the uses of power as well as the misuses—particularly how each may be expressed through the intervening element of his or her personality. What this undeniably implies is that sensitivity to power is essential for successful psychotherapy.

Chapter 10

CONCLUSION
The Power is Thine

The conventional taboo concerning power has until now precluded a greater understanding of its place in the change process. There is a fundamental irony concerning the neglect of power: in light of its ubiquitous presence in psychotherapy even a naive observer would anticipate more professional attention to its understanding. Yet, as indicated by the proceedings of a symposium on social power at the University of Michigan several years ago (see Winter, 1973), the contemporary repression of power is comparable in scope and importance to the nineteenth-century repression of sexuality that, in part, led to the creation of psychotherapy. Even amidst this atmosphere of negativism and denial, however, it is evident from a careful study that power is woven into the very fabric of psychotherapy.

The many origins and manifestations of power in psychotherapy highlight and give life to its underlying role. Power is an essential component for therapy, both as the therapist's contribution to the change process and as the client's intended destination in the search for change. A reasonable amount of power is necessary for an individual client or therapist to become a fully individuated person.

In light of these considerations, we now conclude with a discussion of several facets of psychotherapy and the role of power. Embracing the broadest of psychotherapy concerns, these facets include: (1) the institution of psychotherapy; (2) the technical practice of psychotherapy; and (3) the personal relationship of the participants.

THE INSTITUTION OF PSYCHOTHERAPY

We have seen how power is variously embedded in cultural expectations and ascriptions, in the theories of treatment approach, and in the individual personalities of the participants. We have seen how power is expressed through the structure of the clinical situation, the verbal expressions of the therapist, and the nonverbal communications as well. Finally, we have also observed how power begets therapeutic contributions, and in contrast, triggers therapeutic misuses that threaten the integrity of individual therapies. Yet power extends farther into the heart of the institution of psychotherapy.

As a cornerstone of the therapy process, power reminds us that psychotherapy is essentially a healing institution. The famous Hippocratic oath, which has so profoundly influenced the course of medicine and the medical contribution to psychotherapy, importunes the healing professional "to care for the sick as long as the power is his" (Parloff, 1976). At the same time that this dedication upholds the power of the professional, it clearly denounces self-interest and the abuse of power—owing to its roots in the myth of Aesculapius and its own motifs of power (McLaughlin, 1961). Thus, the medical tradition in psychotherapy, along with its more contemporary variants, entreats all of us to reflect upon power. Above all this tradition demands that the institution of psychotherapy consider its power in relation to those it serves.

Nevertheless, the neglect of therapist power in open discourse continues to engender professional reticence concerning questions of power. In an effort to make psychotherapy appear more scientific and professionally reputable and to divest it from either its primitive healing roots or its negative aura in popular fiction, the field publicly overlooks the more interpersonal curative factors. In so doing, it retreats from acknowledging some of the most compelling elements of change, among which power is undoubtedly prominent.

In spite of an absence of recognition, power trends emerge implicitly in the field and among individual representatives in the field. On one hand, psychotherapy reveals a penchant for a "we have the Word" philosophy. With the individual therapist, this inclination is often expressed by indoctrination into a life perspective related to theoretical treatment approach. With a sense of moral uprightness, a therapist acts with a false aplomb that belies the nature of the profession. He or she inappropriately assumes something of a "therapist's burden," an ascribed mandate to "educate" the uninformed and the unfortunate, may practice psychotherapy with a missionary fervor, and may adopt an unyielding manner concerning theoretical beliefs. This type of therapist is usually not difficult to recognize though the authoritarianism may sometimes be insidious.

The "we have the Word" approach presents precisely the kind of atmosphere that cultivates fear concerning psychotherapy. In such an ambience, there is little choice for a client but to change. However, as Frank (1973) explains, such change accomplished by coercive means is rarely internalized by a client and ordinarily possesses something of an ephemeral quality. Moreover, behind the arrogant facade of "the Word," the individual therapist may live in fear of personal limitations and the shortcomings of the espoused psychological doctrine.

In vivid contrast, psychotherapy also discloses a "lost in the wilderness" tendency. In an individual therapist, this predisposition arises as excessive doubt and powerlessness. Confounded by personal and professional inhibitions, the therapist finds little certainty in human behavior and in the world at large. Expertise and powers of knowledge, faith and comfort are somehow too small. In Peter Shaffer's *Equus*, a psychiatrist's opening soliloquy metaphorically depicts this sense of confusion and futility:

> The thing is, I'm desperate. . . . That's the feeling. All reined up in old language and old assumptions, straining to jump clean-hoofed onto a whole new track of being I only

> suspect is there . . . I can't jump because the bit forbids it,
> and my own basic force—my horsepower, if you like—is
> too little.[1](Shaffer, 1975)

Like Shaffer's troubled psychiatrist, irresolute therapists lack a sense of direction and clarity. They refrain from a prediction with clients because they feel they have no predictive ability. In the course of psychotherapy, they desire to be helpful and appear friendly, but remain pessimistic about real change. As a result, they cast a lingering shadow of doubt.

Along with these opposing inclinations, the institution of psychotherapy also reflects a finely articulated and realistic appreciation of therapeutic power. In individual therapists, this appreciation emerges along with a sense of what can change and what cannot. In the face of this knowledge, they persist in exercising their power for change; at the same time, they ultimately realize that they may have impact only insofar as a client allows change to happen. They are aware that responsibility for change must be shared by both participants (Kaiser, 1955).

While perhaps believing in clinical prediction, consummate therapists know that it is not nearly as accurate as it sometimes seems in the literature. In acknowledging the potential power of the client, such therapists accept their own power and its boundaries. Above all, they continue to remain aware of the changing rhythms of their power urges and fears. In a sense, they follow the lead of Freud, who, in *Analysis Terminable and Interminable*, pleaded for continual self-reflection by the therapist (1937). In moments of quiet reflection, then, sensitive therapists trust that their own personal qualities too will encompass all of the diverse trends that arise in the institution itself.

THE TECHNIQUE OF PSYCHOTHERAPY

Therapist power invests a power of choice in the technical practice of psychotherapy. Early on, our literature review suggested that the concept of power may describe either several different experiences or a single experience manifested in opposing directions. Following an exploration of sources and manifestations, it appears that power is best understood as a unitary social phenomenon applied for disparate purposes, some therapeutic and some not. Thus, it is the application of power within psychotherapeutic technique, and with it the choices over how, when, and what occurs, that are critical to its eventual appearance and impact.

The individual therapist is forever faced with treatment possibilities and must select among them—this is a basic act of therapist power. In any given moment, a question, a suggestion, a comment, or a silent reaction all represent therapeutic alternatives. The response to the moment determines the quality and form that power will take and commences the therapeutic interaction of which power is a part. Azorin (1957), in an article on therapist personality styles, extends this point by suggesting that a therapist is constantly choosing between self-protection and openness to the client.

While individual therapists elect therapeutic decisions continually, therapeutic choices are neither simple nor always conscious (Baum, 1973). On the contrary, there is a constant struggle between helpful therapist interventions and needless or deleterious ones, and the struggle initially emerges just beyond the edge of the therapist's awareness. Therapists must consider multiple levels of their own reactions and multiple layers of ramifications for the client. They must appraise the meaning of their words in terms of the present therapy relationship and in light of the client's other current circumstances (and sometimes past history). While considering numerous therapeutic factors and intervention strategies, the therapist must act or decline to act in a way that is most communicable and effective with the client.

Along with assessing the current state of power, the individual therapist sometimes experiences apprehension associated with a possible misuse of power. He or she must be scrupulous not to use power unwisely and in so doing exacerbate the client's difficulties. For example, Dince (1972) describes the need for a therapist to resist the role of the tyrannical parent, a role that some clients may be all too ready to resurrect. It seems that some clients will steadfastly persist in believing that the therapist is right and superior in all ways; it is absolutely imperative that the therapist not accept this false characterization (Greben, 1975).

However well prepared the repertoire of intervention techniques may be, a therapist must bridge the gap between theory and practice in the sessions with a client. Expertise becomes a double-edged sword when the therapist's carefully-sharpened, incisive capacities are implemented in ill-advised ways.

The gravest applications of power in psychotherapy are reminiscent of the healer's sins in *The Elephant Man*, a widely acclaimed play by Bernard Pomerance.

> The surgeon's hands were well-developed and strong, capable of the most delicate carvings-up, for other's own good
> . . . the right arm was of enormous power, but so incapable of the distinction between the assertion of authority and the charitable act of giving, that it was often to be found disgustingly beating others—for their own good. (1979)[2]

A disturbing glimpse into the misuses of power for certain, *The Elephant Man* speaks in eloquent and exaggerated form to the fear of misdirected power.

Finally, in regard to technique, individual therapists may face tremendous doubt about their power and the power of their treatment approach. Like clients who encounter the ambiguity of the treatment situation, therapists must cope with some degree of ambiguity inherent in their role. Concerned with the stability of their power, therapists can become very absorbed in their limitations and even their powerlessness. Session after session of little discernible client progress inevitably leads to questioning and self-doubt.

In *The Illusionless Man* (1971), psychoanalyst Alan Wheelis describes the therapist's inner doubting: "Where is the poetry of which I am capable?"[3] Yet on occasion, therapist doubt spurs a sense of false conviction as a defense against excessive doubt. Power is misused through a therapist's need for its demonstration. At other times, doubt and apprehension cause a therapist to wallow in an impasse and refrain from effective intervention. Unlike the falsely confident therapist who assumes excessive and misleading power, too little power is assumed by the therapist beleaguered with doubt. Navigating between these contrasting courses, between the absolutism of power on one hand and the impoverishment of power on the other, is as much a part of the practice of psychotherapy as the various intervention techniques themselves.

THE RELATIONSHIP IN PSYCHOTHERAPY

Therapist power also distinguishes the relationship in psychotherapy as a relationship of power. The client's readiness and felt need for power, coupled with the power contributions of the therapist, represent the interpersonal pivot on which the psychotherapeutic relationship turns. By its very presence, therapist power suggests that a change in power is fundamental for client change and that therapeutic relationships represent a forum for the unfolding of power dynamics. As Strupp (1976) asserts concerning the nature of therapeutic influence, a matrix of virtually unparalleled interpersonal power is created in psychotherapy and it is within this matrix that a therapist has the opportunity to achieve unique effectiveness.

At the outset of the psychotherapy relationship, clients enter with a relative deficiency or an absence of power. Often, they seek psychotherapy precisely because of the overwhelming power of their predicament, the troubles and fears that they seemingly cannot escape. Their problems frequently reflect a peculiar tenacity. They experience themselves as powerless, able only to ask: "What is to be done?"

The therapist, on the other hand, symbolizes to both participants the power to ameliorate or resolve these previously intractable problems (Frank, 1959). He or she originates as a new force to be reckoned with, a figure called up to oppose the powerful and debilitating circumstances of the client's life. Therapist power, in the therapeutic relationship and in interventions which enliven the relationship, constitutes the leverage for the behavioral or intrinsic advances of the client.

As a consequence of psychotherapy's interpersonal ground plan, much of the duration of most psychotherapies reflects an imbalance of power: the therapist is clearly the powerholder. Given a client's initial circumstances, he or she tends to locate greater power in the therapist and require a therapist to personify such power. What then follows is often a considerable ebb and flow of, and even struggle over, power throughout the course of therapy. Depending on the length of the therapy and the nature of the client's problems, the imbalance may be minimal or substantial. Nevertheless, power is what the client needs help with and power is expected to reside in the therapist's chair. Therapist Donald Broughton speaks to the changing tide of power in psychotherapy:

> In therapy, a person must come to the point of abandoning his drowning mode of struggling and move to a struggle that uses the strength of the relationship. He must be willing to let go of a part of himself that he has cherished, namely the myth of his own total sufficiency. At this juncture with a person, a therapist must be willing to ride with his or her own authority. (Stern, 1981, p. 31)

In a modal intensive psychotherapy, for example, an evaluation stage usually unveils the client's doubts and fears about therapy and signals the therapist initially to demonstrate some evidence of power. The therapist may attempt to allay some of the client's misgivings and to arouse the client's hope. Still early on, a therapist ordinarily enacts the power of the clinical approach and confronts the client's reluctance or resistance to receive help. Here, as well, the impact is largely one-sided. Power is vested in the therapist and the client is either influenced or avoids influence. Just as in life outside of therapy, the client exerts little impact over personal troubles or in the therapy process. Mann (1973) sees these initial interviews as critically powerful in the development of a good therapeutic relationship and in the establishment of a therapeutic approach.

As the therapy progresses to a middle period, the therapeutic relationship tends to acquire greater depth (depending on the type of therapy) as the set of treatment techniques is presented. The opportunity for power struggles is ripe and power conflict is commonplace. Sometimes out of the fear of power and the fear of change, a client may react against even the genuinely helpful efforts of the therapist. The client seeks to achieve a more equal posture, even if at first this means only to exercise the privilege of remaining anchored in an existing, debilitating life style.

Ultimately, during the closing stages, the *raison d'etre* for most therapies emerges as a balance of power in the relationship. Therapist and client share in the therapeutic work and mutually influence each other. In therapies of high therapist ambiguity, there may be greater personal disclosure by the therapist and greater acknowledgment of the realistic boundaries of power. Outside the therapeutic context, balance implies a realization that both individuals are part of the same life process and share in the human situation. Rowan (1976), speaking of power from a sociological perspective, maintains that power is ordinarily a "two-way" thing if each party is aware of the other's expectations and values. With open communication, Rowan contends, power can become more of "a process of negotiation than domination" (1976).

While a balance of power may be optimal and finally tenable at the conclusion of a successful therapy, therapists must preserve this goal in mind throughout. When they become blind to a common potential for power, then they falter and lay themselves vulnerable to the misuses of power. When mindful of the need for balance, they then encourage a therapy relationship that can nurture a transformation in their clients from powerlessness to personal ascendancy.

Finally, the therapeutic relationship must result in an emerging acceptance of personal power by the client. This is, after all, the essential goal of many psychotherapies—to achieve for the client a greater level of personal integration and freedom. Rollo May (1979) speaks emphatically about the role of power in psychotherapy.

> The acquisition of power, the power within one's self and the awareness that one can influence other people, is absolutely essential to the confidence and mental health of a person. (p. 142)

The newfound power of the client resembles the therapist's power to some extent, as an outgrowth of their relationship, but it also retains its own uniqueness. Setting out with insufficient power, ideally clients gain through psychotherapy a sense of their own impact and the potential to determine their own fate. In the most involved and successful of therapies, the power of the self for the client arises along with a greater knowledge of the self, of one's aspirations as well as one's limitations.[4]

Concluding Thoughts

In the final picture, therapeutic power offers neither the definitive answer nor merely a vague indication for pain and its cure. When the guise of unspoken taboo is lifted from therapeutic power, it paradoxically resembles that power for which the client also searches. This is the human power of personal will. It is the power of faith in an ability to relate and intervene with others, a power of hope that together the pair will succeed in the shared therapeutic endeavor. It is a power that stands in the face of life's uncertainty, and all too often, encounters a past history and a therapeutic challenge that promise to be formidable in their own right.

The therapist's power may also be thought of as a gateway to freedom, a passage for the previously troubled person toward greater strength and vision, for without power, there can be no freedom. Therapeutic power is perhaps what the philosopher Emerson intended when he spoke of "a victorious poise of mind," the fertile and necessary ground for personal freedom (Baudoin, 1923).

Each individual seeks his or her own conception of freedom in psychotherapy, whether freedom means emancipation from learned fears or from parental directives. While the visions and troubles of individuals may differ, these differences are not as significant as the common process each experiences.

What is vital in psychotherapy, then, is that two individuals be willing to struggle together in a relationship fraught with power. They must be willing to sift through the many hidden sources and expressions of power so that freedom may emerge. The outcome, if they are successful, may be as profound as a rediscovery of their creative and loving possibilities. Since so many people seem to enter psychotherapy because of an inability to create and to love, it is perhaps understandable that a particularly power-laden encounter is necessary to change the course of their lives. In its best and most soulful form, this is the nature of power in psychotherapeutic practice.

NOTES

CHAPTER 1

1. In person perception research, this notion is sometimes called "relevance," defined as a circumstance under which the actor's behavior does have consequences for the observer (Jones & Davis, 1965).

2. The sequencing of affects and thoughts is a source of current and historical controversy in psychology. Zajonc (1980) provides a compelling argument for the primacy of feelings and summarizes some of the competing arguments. A major philosophical voice in the contemporary literature is Susanne Langer, whose book *Mind: An Essay on Human Feeling*, Volume I (1967) asserts that knowledge is a development out of feeling.

3. In *Love, Power and Justice* (1954), theologian Paul Tillich argues for a close relationship between power and love and yet offers an inter-theological differentiation between the two.

CHAPTER 2

1. Freud introduced the topic in his *Recommendations to physicians practicing psychoanalysis* (1912). Standard Edition, 12:111-120.

2. "Client" will ordinarily be used to refer to the recipient of psycho-therapy. "Patient" will sometimes appear in this discussion in conjunction with psychoanalysis or hospital-related psychotherapy.

3. A further reference to Freud's warning against countertransference and its potentially disturbing effects, *verboten* accents the "forbidden" ambience surrounding therapist reactions.

4. Winnicott provides some insightful illustrations of the dilemma faced by many therapists with regard to hate reactions. He quips that a common thought for a therapist in the throes of hate might be: "I should not feel hate because I get paid for this" (1949).

5. From Freud's *The future prospects for psychoanalytic therapy* (1910). Standard Edition 11:141-151.

6. Some in the literature call this "R," a term to denote the total response of a therapist to his client (Little, 1957).

7. Little (1967) provides an interesting and commendable piece on the course of therapy following a psychotherapist's heart attack.

CHAPTER 3

1. Kopp's quotation appears in *If You Find the Buddha on the Road, Kill Him!* (1972), a perceptive essay on psychotherapy as a personal journey. Kopp compares the guide role of psychotherapy to the guide phenomenon in Eastern philosophy societies.

2. The relationship between knowledge and power is most common-place in our thinking owing to Sir Francis Bacon's well-known adage: "Knowledge is power" (1597).

3. There are similar expectations of guide figures in particular cultural groups. In traditional Jewish lore, for example, this figure is called a *zaddik*. Similar to his modern-day therapy counterpart, the *zaddik* is expected to heal body and mind. His special art is perceiving how heaven and earth are bound up with each other. As a result of the power derived from his knowledge the *zaddik* assumes a coveted place in the culture (Buber, 1947).

CHAPTER 4

1. Lennard and Bernstein (1960) note that such a singular focus is quite common among role induction methods in general, even outside of the psychotherapy setting.

2. Chethik (1969) also discusses a therapist's powerlessness in working with children, a sense that one can only "pick up the pieces." Chethik observes that the developmental level of the client enhances the intensity of this reaction for the therapist and can cause considerable emotional "wear and tear."

CHAPTER 5

1. Friedman and Dies (1974), for instance, explored the relationship between therapist style (directive vs. nondirective) and client locus of control (internal vs. external). In their experimental paradigm, the authors presented two forms of behavioral tasks and nondirective counseling each on a continuum of therapist directiveness, a variable related to power and degree of influence. Results suggested that high directiveness therapists were more effective with high external clients; low directiveness therapists showed better outcomes with high internal clients. The authors concluded that therapist directiveness was a critical therapist variable when considered in conjunction with similarly important client variables like locus of control.

2. Love et al. (1972) report that important individual differences may exist in response to very directed interventions. Specifically, lower socioeconomic status parents and children respond more favorably to directive intervention and higher economic status parents respond in an opposite fashion. Issues of personal autonomy, it seems, may moderate individual reaction to influencing and modeling attempts.

CHAPTER 6

1. Braatoy (1954) is emphatic concerning the diverse uses of the couch, commenting, ". . . the couch is an instrument, not a commandment . . ." If the therapist does not abuse the overseeing position, Braatoy suggests, the couch can reveal hidden conflict through the blockage of spontaneous movement by the client. Thus, it seems that as a technical addition to the setting, the couch can enhance a therapist's access to information and help to support the power of knowledge.

Braatoy also sees the chair as symbolizing acceptance and comfort along with its technical value. This is intended to foster in the patient the belief and faith that he or she will not receive harsh treatment or rejection.

2. *The Manticore* (1972) is the second novel in a trilogy by Robertson Davies.

3. Hiatt (1978) notes a therapist's particular control and potential mishandling of time during the termination of psychotherapy.

CHAPTER 7

1. From anthropological linguistics, the study of Brown and Gilman (1962) argues persuasively for a close relationship between power ideology and pronoun semantics. Historically, the roots of the European formal pronoun of address and the American formal title can be discovered in the courts of emperors and priests of the Middle Ages. Eventually, such titles were bestowed upon more familiar power figures, parents, and elder relations.

2. Even when the content of recorded speech is nearly obliterated, experimental participants can still reliably encode emotions expressed in speech (Argyle, 1970; Dawes & Kramer, 1966).

CHAPTER 8

1. Whitman et al. (1969) present Freud's famous dream of his patient Irma. The authors discuss how discovery of illegitimate power, the desire "to reproach her for not having accepted my solution yet," helped Freud in the analysis with Irma.

CHAPTER 9

1. With regard to therapist expectancies, Zajonc and Brickman (1969) note that experiences have both cognitive and motivational factors and, much like aspirations, tend to act as outcome goals. Thus one might speculate that a therapist's expectancies play no small role in the therapeutic interaction and outcome.

2. Baron (1960) presents a parallel use of practitioners' reactions in the classroom setting. He observes that teachers' responses to specific individuals or children in general can be used to explain classroom interaction patterns.

3. R. Butler et al. (1968) provide some empirical support for the effectiveness of therapist expression in client-centered therapies.

4. The obvious implication which underlies the induction of powerlessness is that therapists fear their own sense of powerlessness. Thus they need to locate such a feeling in the client. On a sociological level, this view appears in Franz Fanon's *Wretched of the Earth* (1963). Fanon argues that historical moments which render individuals ineffectual and powerless stir these individuals to use coercion when attempting to influence others.

5. On extreme power reactions which are client-provoked, Theodore Rubin writes: "When patients insist on believing that their analyst is dominant, powerful, aggressive, and even tyrannical, it is often because they desire to use the analyst to put down the tyrant in themselves" (1976).

6. Frank (1973) compares the imposition of values in psychotherapy with political thought reform. Sometimes, he seems to contend, clients identify with this illegitimate application of power and become "its obedient instrument," forcing themselves on significant others in a similarly inappropriate manner. The therapist, in helping the client to become a more effective person, demonstrates to the client the "error of his ways" so that he can rejoin the society and communicate the therapeutic teachings.

CHAPTER 10

1. *Equus* (Shaffer, 1975) is a psychodrama concerning the treatment of a boy who attacks a stable full of horses. The play offers much insight into the inner tribulations of the psychotherapist and his relationship with the passions of his client.

2. *The Elephant Man* (Pomerance, 1979) is of course based on the medical and psychological care of John Merrick, who suffered from gross physical abnormalities.

3. *The Illusionless Man* (Wheelis, 1971) is a therapist's reflections on man's struggle with himself both in and out of psychotherapy.

4. Harold Searles (1975) argues that eventually a patient may become a kind of therapist to himself and others and needs to discover this. Searles explains ". . . innate among man's most powerful strivings to-

ward his fellow man, beginning in the earliest years and even the earliest months of life, is an essentially psychotherapeutic striving . . . . the patient is ill because, and to the degree that [his own psychotherapeutic strivings have been frustrated]."

REFERENCES

Aaron, R. The analyst's emotional life during work. *Journal of the American Psychoanalytic Association*, 1974, *22*, 160-169.

Abse, D., & Ewing, J. Transference and countertransference in somatic therapies. *Journal of Nervous and Mental Disease*, 1956, *123*,32.

Adler, A. *Understanding human nature*. New York: Greenburg Press, 1927.

Adler, G., & Buie, D. The misuses of confrontation with the borderline patient. In LeBoit and Cappori (Eds.). *Advances in psychotherapy of the borderline patient*. New York: Jason Aronson, 1979.

Akeret, R. *Not by words alone*. New York: Wylie, 1972.

Alger, I. The clinical handling of the analyst's responses. *Psychoanalytic Forum*, 1966, *I*,289-297.

Argyle, M. *The psychology of interpersonal behavior*. Middlesex, England: Penguin, Ltd., 1967.

Azorin, L. The analyst's personal equation. *American Journal of Psychoanalysis*, 1957, *17*,34-38.

Bacon, F. Meditations sacrae. *De Haeresibus*, 1597.

Bahnson, C. Nonverbal behavior in psychotherapy. In S. Carson & E. Corson (Eds.). *Ethology and nonverbal communication*. Oxford: Pergamon Press, 1980.

Balint, M. Analytic training and training analysts. *Journal of the American Psychoanalytic Association*, 1951, *1*,157.

Balint, A., & Balint, M. On transference and countertransference. *International Journal of Psychoanalysis*, 1939, *20*,223-230.

Baranger, M., & Baranger, W. Insight in the analytic situation. In J. Masserman (Ed.). *The dynamics of power*. New York: Grune & Stratton, 1972.

Barchilon, J. On countertransference "cures." *Journal of American Psychological Association*, 1958, *6*,222-236.

Baron, R. *Human aggression*. New York: Plenum Press, 1977.

Baron, S. Transference and countertransference in the classroom. *Psychoanalysis and Psychoanalytic Review*, 1960, *47*,76-96.

Barton, A. *Three worlds of therapy*. New York: National Press Books, 1974.

Baudoin, C. *The power within us*. E. Paul & C. Paul, trans. Freeport, New York: Libraries Press, 1923.

Baum, E. Further thoughts on countertransference. *Psychoanalytic Review*, 1973, *60*,1, 127-140.

———. Countertransference. *Psychoanalytic Review*, 1969-70, *56*, 621-637.

Bellak, L. Free association: Conceptual and clinical aspects. *International Journal of Psychoanalysis*, 1961, *42*,9-20.

Benedek, T. Dynamics of the countertransference. *Bulletin of the Menninger Clinic*, 1953, *17*,201.

Beres, D., & Arlow, J. Fantasy and identification in empathy. *Psychoanalytic Quarterly*, 1974, *43*,1, 26-50.

Berkowitz, L. *Roots of aggression*. New York: Atherton Press, 1969.

Berman, L. Countertransference and attitudes of the analyst in the therapeutic process. *Psychiatry*, 1949, *12*,159-166.

Bernstein, A. The problem of the transference in psychoanalysis. *Psychoanalysis and Psychoanalytic Review*, 1958, *45*,85-91.

Bernstein, L., & Burris, B. *The contribution of the social sciences to psychotherapy*. Springfield, Ill.: Thomas Publishers, 1967.

Bettelheim, B. Freud and the soul. In *The New Yorker*, March 19, 1982, 52.

Bieber, I. Sex and power. In J. Masserman (Ed.). *The dynamics of power*. New York: Grune & Stratton, 1972.

Bierstadt, R. An analysis of social power. *American Sociological Review*, 1950, *6*,7-30.

Bordin, E. *Research strategies in psychotherapy.* New York: Wiley, 1974.

———. *Psychological counseling.* New York: Appleton-Century, 1968.

Braatoy, T. *Fundamentals of psychoanalytic technique.* New York: Wiley, 1954.

Brehm, S. *The application of social psychology to clinical practice.* New York: Wiley & Sons, 1976.

Brehm, S., & Brehm, S. *Psychological resistance: A theory of freedom and control.* New York: Academic Press, 1981.

Brink, T. *Geriatric psychotherapy.* New York: Human Sciences Press, 1979.

Brockbank, R. On the analyst's silence in psychoanalysis: A synthesis of intrapsychic content and interpersonal manifestation. *International Journal of Psychoanalysis,* 1970, *51*,457-464.

Bromberg, W. *The nature of psychotherapy: A critique of psychotherapeutic transaction.* New York: Grune & Stratton, 1962.

Brown, R., & Gilman, A. The pronouns of power and solidarity. *Anthropological Linguistics,* 1962, *IV* (6),24-29.

Buber, M. *Tales of the Hasidim: Early masters.* New York: Schocken Books, 1947.

Burton, A. *The patient and the therapist: New light on the psychotherapist.* Sacramento: Hamilton Psyche Press, 1975.

Butler, R., & Rice, M. Therapist expressiveness and patient progress. Cited in E. Bordin, *Psychological Counseling.* New York: Appleton-Century, 1968.

Cain, A. Therapist response to client resistance. Doctoral thesis, University of Michigan, 1962.

Chetnik, M. The emotional "wear and tear" of child therapy. Reprinted from the *Smith College Studies in Social Work,* February 1969.

Christies, R., & Geis, F. *Studies in Machiavellianism.* New York: Academic Press, 1971.

Clark, K. The pathos of power. *American Psychologist,* 1971, *26*,1047-57.

Cohen, A. Situational structure, self-esteem and threat-oriented reactions to power. In D. Cartwright (Ed.). *Studies in social power,* Ann Arbor: The University of Michigan, 1959.

Cohen, A., Terry, H., & Jones, C. Attitudinal effects of choice in exposure to counterpropaganda. *Journal of Abnormal and Social Psychology,* 1959, *58*,388-391.

Cohen, M. Countertransference and anxiety. *Psychiatry,* 1952, *15*,231-243.

Cutler, R. Countertransference effects in psychotherapy. *Journal of Consulting Psychology*, 1958, *22*,349-356.

Davies, R. *The Manticore*. New York: Penguin Books, 1972.

Dawes, R., & Kramer, E. A proximity analysis of vocally expressed emotion. *Perceptual and Motor Skills*, 1966, *22*:571-574.

Dean, E. Drowsiness as a symptom of countertransference. *Psychoanalytic Quarterly*, 1957, *25*,246-247.

DeCharms, R. *Personal causation*. New York: Academic Press, 1968.

Deutsch, F. Thus speaks the body, analytic posturology. *Psychoanalytic Quarterly*, 1951, *20*,338-339.

Dince, P. Power and omnipotence. In J. Masserman (Ed.). *The dynamics of power*. New York: Grune & Stratton, 1972.

Ekman, P., & Friesen, W. Nonverbal behavior. In P. Ostwald (Ed.). *Communication and social interaction*. New York: Grune & Stratton, 1977.

Ekstein, R. Concerning the teaching and learning of psychoanalysis. *Journal of American Psychoanalysis Association*, 1969, *17*,1.

Ellis, A. Rational emotive therapy. In R. Corsini (Ed.). *Current psychotherapies*. Hasca, Ill.: Peacock Publications, 1973.

Erikson, F. Talking down: Some cultural sources of miscommunication in interracial interviews. In A. Wolfgang (Ed.). *Nonverbal behavior: Applications and cultural implications*. New York: Academic Press, 1980.

Fanon, F. *The wretched of the earth*. New York: Grove Press, 1963.

Fast, J. *Body politics: How to get power with class*. New York: Tower Books, 1963.

Feldstein, S. Temporal patterns of dialogue: Basic research and considerations. In A. Siegman & B. Pope (Eds.). *Studies in dyadic communication*. New York: Pergamon Press, 1972.

Fenichel, O. *Problems of psychoanalytic technique*. D. Brunswick, trans. New York: Psychoanalytic Quarterly Press, 1941.

Ferenczi, S. The elasticity of psycho-analytic technique. In S. Ferenczi (Ed.). *Final contributions to the problems and methods of psychoanalysis*. New York: Basic Books, 1928.

——. On the technique of psycho-analysis. In *First considerations to the technique of psycho-analysis*. London: Hogarth Press, 1919.

Feshbach, S. *Aggression and behavior change: Biological and social processes*. New York: Praeger, 1979.

Fordham, M. Countertransference. *British Journal of Medical Psychology*, 1960, *33*,1-8.

Forisha, B. *Power and love: How to work for success and still care for others.* New Jersey: Prentice-Hall, 1982.

Frank, J. *Persuasion and healing.* New York: Schocken Books, 1973.

Frankl, V. *The doctor and the soul: From psychotherapy to logotherapy.* New York: Knopf, 1965.

Freedman, D. The survival value of beards. *Psychology Today,* 3 October 1969, 38.

French, J., & Raven, B. The bases of social power. In D. Cartwright (Ed.). *Studies in social power.* Ann Arbor: University of Michigan Press, 1959.

Freud, S. Analysis terminable and interminable. *Standard Edition,* 1937, *23*,209-253.

————. Recommendations to physicians practicing psychoanalysis. *Standard Edition,* 1912, *11*,111-120.

————. The future prospects for psychoanalytic therapy. *Standard Edition,* 1910, *11*,141-151.

Friedman, L. The therapeutic alliance. *International Journal of Psychoanalysis,* 1969, *50*,139-153.

Friedman, M., & Dies, R. Reactions of internal and external test-anxious students to counseling and behavior therapies. *Journal of Consulting and Clinical Psychology,* 1974, *42*,921.

Fromm-Reichmann, F. *Principles of intensive psychotherapy.* Chicago: University of Chicago Press, 1950.

Gadpaille, W. The uses of power: A particular impasse in psychoanalysis. In J. Masserman (Ed.). *The dynamics of power,* New York: Grune & Stratton, 1972.

Gedo, J. Forms of idealization in the analytic transference. *Journal of the American Psychoanalytic Association,* 1975, *23*:485-506.

Gelb, L. Psychotherapy as a redistribution of power. In J. Masserman (Ed.). *The dynamics of power.* New York: Grune & Stratton, 1972.

Giovacchini, P. The many sides of helplessness: The borderline patient. In LeBoit & Cappori (Eds.). *Advances in psychotherapy of the borderline patient.* New York: Jason Aronson, 1979.

Gitelson, M. The curative factors in psychoanalysis: The first phase of psychoanalysis. *International Journal of Psychoanalysis,* 1962, *43*, 194-205.

Goldin, G., et al. *Dependency and its implications for rehabilitation.* Lexington: Heath & Co., 1972.

Goldstein, A., Heller, K., & Sechrest, L. *Psychotherapy and the psychology of behavior change.* New York: Wiley & Sons, 1966.

Greenson, R. Loving, hating and indifference toward the patient. *International Review of Psychoanalysis*, 1974, *1*,259-266.

————. *The technique and practice of psychoanalysis.* New York: International University Press Inc., 1967.

Greenspoon, J. The reinforcing effects of two spoken sounds on the frequency of two responses. *American Journal of Psychology*, 1955, *68*,409-416.

Grudin, R. *Mighty opposites: Shakespeare and Renaissance contrariety.* Berkeley: University of California Press, 1979.

Guntrip, H. My experience of analysis with Fairbairn and Winnicott. *International Review of Psychoanalysis*, 1975, 2:145.

Haak, N. Comments on the analytic situation. *International Journal of Psycho-Analysis*, 1957, *38*,183-195.

Haley, J. The art of psychoanalysis (1958). In *The power tactics of Jesus Christ and other essays.* New York: Grossman, 1969.

Hall, E. Listening behavior: Some cultural differences. *Phi Delta Kappan*, 1969, *50*,370-380.

Harris, L. Psychopolitics: Feminist therapy in the '80's. *The Village Voice*, Vol. XXVII, No. 10, March 9, 1982.

Heller, K. Ambiguity in the interview situation. In J. Schlien (Ed.). *Research in psychotherapy* (Vol. II). Washington, D.C.: American Psychological Association, 1968.

Henry, W. Personal and social identities of psychotherapists. In A. Gurman & A. Razin (Eds.). *Effective psychotherapy.* Oxford: Penguin, 1977.

Hiatt, H. The problem of termination in psychotherapy. *American Journal of Psychotherapy*, 1978, 607.

Hillman, J., & Goethals, G. Social responsibility and threat to behavioral freedom as determinants of altruistic behavior. *Journal of Personality*, 1973, *41*,376-384.

Hoffman, L. Effects of the employment of mothers on parental power relations and the division of household tasks. *Marriage and Family Living*, 1960, *22*,27-35.

Izard, C., & Tomkins, S. (Eds.). *Affect, cognition and personality.* New York: Springer, 1965.

Jackson, A. Psychotherapy: Factors associated with the race of the therapist. *Psychotherapy: Theory, Research and Practice*, 1973, *10*,273-277.

Jacobs, R. Posture, gesture and movement in the analyst: Cues to interpretation and countertransference. *Journal of the American Psychological Association*, 1973, *21*,77-92.

Jones, E., & Davis, K. From acts to dispositions: The attribution process in person perception. In L. Berkowitz (Ed.). *Advances in experimental psychology* (Vol. 2). New York: Academic Press, 1965.

Jourard, S., & Jaffee, P. Influence of an interviewer's disclosures on the self-disclosing behavior of interviewees. *Journal of Counseling Psychology*, 1970, *17*,252-257.

Kaiser, H. The problem of responsibility in psychotherapy. *Psychiatry*, 1955, *18*,205-211.

Kempler, W. Gestalt therapy. In R. Corsini (Ed.). *Current Psychotherapies*, Ibasca, Ill.: Research Publications, 1973.

Kern, J. Countertransference and spontaneous screens. *Journal of the American Psychoanalytic Association*, 1978, *26*,1.

Kernberg, O. Factors in the psychoanalytic treatment of narcissistic personalities. *Journal of the American Psychoanalytic Association*, 1970, *18*,51-85.

———. Notes on countertransference. *Journal of the American Psychoanalytic Association*, 1965, *13*,137-158.

Khan, M. On symbiotic omnipotence. *Psychoanalytic Forum*, 1969, *3*,137-158.

Kipnis, D. The powerholder. In J. Tedeschi (Ed.). *Perspectives on social power*. Chicago: Aldine Publishing, 1974.

Klein, M., Dittman, A., Parloff, M., & Gill, M. Behavior therapy: Observations and reflections. *Journal of Consulting and Clinical Psychology*, 1969, *33*,259-266.

Kohut, H. The psychoanalytic treatment of narcissistic personality disorders: Outline of a systematic approach. *Psychoanalytic Study of the Child*, 1968, *23*,86-113.

Kopp, S. *An end to innocence: Facing life without illusions.* New York: MacMillan Publishing Co., 1978.

———. *If you meet the Buddha on the road, kill him!* Ben Lomond, Calif.: Science and Behavior Books, 1972.

Krumboldtz, J., Vavenhovst, B., & Thoresen, C. Nonverbal factors in the effectiveness of modes in counseling. *Journal of Counseling Psychology*, 1967, *14*,412-418.

LaCrosse, M. Nonverbal behavior and perceived counselor attractiveness and persuasiveness. *Journal of Counseling Psychology*, 1975, *22*(6):563-566.

Lambert, M., Bergin, A., & Collins, J. Therapist-induced deterioration in psychotherapy. In A. Gruman & A. Razin (Eds.). *Effective psychotherapy*. Oxford: Pergamon Press, 1977.

Langer, Susanne. *Mind: An essay on human feeling* (Vol. 1). Baltimore: Johns Hopkins Press, 1967.

Langs, R. *The bipersonal field.* New York: Jason Aronson, 1976.

Lasswell, H. *Power and personality.* New York: W. W. Norton, 1955.

Lazarus, A. *Behavior therapy and beyond.* New York: McGraw-Hill, 1971.

Lennard, H., & Bernstein, A. *The anatomy of psychotherapy: Systems of communications and expectation.* New York: Columbia University Press, 1960.

Levinson, D. *The seasons of a man's life.* New York: Knopf, 1978.

Lewin, K. *Field theory in social science: Selected theoretical papers.* D. Cartwright (Ed.). New York: Harper, 1951.

Lieberman, D. Affective response of the analyst to the patient's communications. *International Journal of Psycho-Analysis,* 1978, *59*,335.

Lindner, R. *The fifty-minute hour.* New York: Bantam Books, 1955.

Little, M. The analyst's total response to his patient's needs. *International Journal of Psychoanalysis,* 1957, *32*,240-254.

Love, L., et al. Differential effects of three clinical interviews for different socioeconomic groupings. *Journal of Consulting and Clinical Psychology,* 1972, *39*,347-360.

McClelland, D. *Power: The inner experience.* New York: Irvington Publishing Co., 1975.

———. The two faces of power. In D. McClelland & R. Steele (Eds.). *Human motivation.* Morristown, N.J.: General Learning Press, 1973.

McGlaughlin, J. The sleepy analyst: Some observations on states of consciousness in the analyst at work. *Journal of the American Psychoanalytic Association,* 1975, *23*,106-125.

———. The analyst and the Hippocratic oath. *Journal of the American Psychoanalytic Association,* 1961, *9*,106-123.

MacCauley, J., & Berkowitz, L. *Altruism and helping behavior.* New York: Academic Press, 1970.

Machiavelli Writings (1640). Introduction, H. Crust. London: D. Nutt, 1905.

Malan, D. *The frontier of brief psychotherapy.* New York: Plenum, 1976.

Malcolm, J. *The impossible profession.* New York: Random House, 1980.

Mann, J. *Time-limited psychotherapy.* Cambridge: Harvard University Press, 1973.

Markus, H. The self in thought and memory. In D. Wegner & R. Vallacher (Eds.). *The self in social psychology,* Oxford: Oxford University Press, 1980.

Masserman, J. (Ed.). *The dynamics of power.* New York: Grune & Stratton, 1972.

Matarazzo, J., Wiens, A., Saslow, G., & Weitman, M. Interviewer head nodding and interviewer speech durations. *Psychotherapy: Theory, Research and Practice,* 1964, *1,*109-114.

May, R. Psychoanalysis and power. In Donald Harward (Ed.). *Power: Its nature, its use and its limits.* Boston: Hall & Co., 1979.

————. *Power and innocence.* New York: W. W. Norton, 1972.

————. *Love and will.* New York: W. W. Norton, 1969.

Medoff, M. *Children of a lesser God.* Clifton, N.J.: White & Co., 1980.

Mehrabian, A., & Williams, M. Nonverbal concomitants of perceived and intended persuasiveness. *Journal of Personality and Social Psychology,* 1969, *13,*37-58.

Money-Kryle, R. Normal countertransference and some of its deviations. *International Journal of Psycho-Analysis,* 1956, *37,*360-366.

Moos, J., & Clemens, S. Therapist-patient interactions. Cited in *Ethology and nonverbal communication in mental health.* Oxford: Pergamon Press, 1980.

Moser, T. *Years of apprenticeships on the couch.* New York: Urizen Books, 1977.

Murray, E., & Jacobson, L. The nature of learning in traditional and behavioral psychotherapy. In A. Berger & S. Garfield (Eds.). *Handbook of psychotherapy and behavior change: An empirical analysis.* New York: Wiley, 1967.

Nacht, S. Interference between transference and countertransference. In M. Schur (Ed.). *Drives, affects, behavior* (Vol. 2). New York: International Universities Press, 1965.

Nelson, M. *Roles and paradigms in psychotherapy.* New York: Grune & Stratton, 1968.

Orr, D. Transference and countertransference: An historical survey. *Journal of the American Psychoanalytic Association,* 1954, *2,*621-670.

Parents, H, & Saul, L. *Dependence in man.* New York: International Universities Press, 1971.

Perls, F. *The gestalt approach and eye witness to therapy.* Ben Lomond, Calif.: Science and Behavior Books, 1973.

Pomerance, B. *The elephant man.* New York: Grove Press, 1979.

Porter, L. Communication: Structure and process. In H. Fromkin & J. Sherwood (Eds.). *Integrating the organization: A social psychological analysis.* New York: Free Press, 1974.

Prochaska, J. *Systems of psychotherapy*. Homewood, Ill.: Dorsey Press, 1979.

Racker, H. The meaning and uses of countertransference. *Psychoanalytic Quarterly*, 1957, *25*,303-357.

———. Counterresistance and interpetation. *Journal of the American Psychoanalytic Association*, 1956, *4*,215.

Raimy, V. *Misunderstanding of the self*. San Francisco: Jossey-Bass, 1975.

Reich, A. Empathy and countertransference. In *Psychoanalytic contributions*. New York: International Universities Press, Inc., 1966.

———. On countertransference. *International Journal of Psychoanalysis*, 1951, *32*,25-31.

Reik, T. *Listening with the third ear: The inner experience of a psychoanalyst*. New York: Farrar, Straus, 1948.

Roe, A. Individual motivation and personal factors in career choice. In F. Arnhoff (Ed.). *Manpower for mental health* Chicago: Aldine, 1969.

Rogers, C. A dialogue between therapists. In C. Rogers (Ed.). *The therapeutic relationship and its impact: A study of psychotherapy with schizophrenics*. Madison, Wis.: University of Wisconsin Press, 1967.

Rollins, B., & Thomas, D. A theory of parental power and child compliance. In R. Cromwell & D. Olsen (Eds.). *Power in the family*. New York: Halsted Press, 1975.

Rosenthal, D., & Frank, J. Psychotherapy and the placebo effect. *Psychological Bulletin*, 1956, *53*,294-302.

Rowan, John. *The power of the group*. London: Davis-Poynter, 1976.

Rubin, T. *Love me, love my fool: Thoughts from a psychoanalyst's notebook*. New York: McKay Company, Inc., 1976.

———. *In the life*. New York: MacMillan, 1961.

Ruesch, J. *Therapeutic communication*. New York: W. W. Norton, 1961.

Russell, B. *Power: A new social analysis*. New York: W. W. Norton, 1938.

Salzman, L. Psychotherapy with the obsessive personality. In T. Karksu & L. Bellah (Eds.). *Specialized techniques in individual psychotherapy*, New York: Bruner-Mazel, 1980.

———. Compulsive drives for power. In J. Masserman (Ed.). *The dynamics of power*. New York: Grune & Stratton, 1972.

Sampson, R. *Equality and power*. London: Heineman Publishers, 1965.

Sandler, J., Holder, A., & Dure, C. Basic psychoanalytic concepts: IV. Countertransference. *British Journal of Psychiatry*, 1970, *117*,83-88.

Sattler, J. The effects of therapist-client racial similarity. In A. Gurman & A. Razin (Eds.). *Effective psychotherapy*, Oxford: Penguin, 1977.

r, S., & Singer, J. Cognitive, social and physiological determi-
nts of emotional state. *Psychological Review*, 1962, *65*,379-399.

Sch..len, A. *Communicational structure: Analysis of a psychotherapy transaction*. Bloomington, Ind.: University Press, 1973.

Schimel, J. The relevance of power: An introduction. In J. Masserman (Ed.). *The dynamics of power*. New York: Grune & Stratton, 1972.

Schopler, J., & Layton, B. Attributions of interpersonal power. In J. Tedeschi (Ed.). *Perspectives on social power*. Chicago: Aldine, 1974.

Schulman, J., Kaspar, J., & Barger, P. *The therapeutic dialogue*. Springfield, Ill.: Thomas Publishing Co., 1964.

Searles, H. The patient as therapist to his analyst. In P. Giovacchini (Ed.). *Tactics and techniques in psychoanalytic therapy* (Vol. II): *Countertransference*. New York: Jason Aronson, 1975.

———. The schizophrenic's vulnerability to the therapist's unconscious processes. *Journal of Nervous and Mental Disease*, 1958, *127*,247-262.

Sequin, C. *Love and psychotherapy: The psychotherapeutic eros*. New York: Litra, 1965.

Shaffer, P. *Equus*. New York: Atheneum, 1975.

Shakespeare, W. *The Tempest* (1670). Printed by New York: Dover, 1964.

Sherman, M. Peripheral cues and invisible countertransference. In M. Nelson (Ed.). *Roles and paradigms in psychotherapy*. New York: Grune & Stratton, 1968.

Singer, B., & Luborsky, L. Countertransference: The status of clinical versus quantitative research. In E. A. Gurman & A. Razin (Eds.). *Effective psychotherapy*. Oxford: Pergamon Press, 1977.

Skinner, B. F. *Walden Two*. New York: MacMillan Co., 1948.

Sloane, R. Short-term analytically oriented therapy versus behavior therapy. Paper presented at the *Fifth Annual Meeting of the Society of Psychotherapy Research*, Denver, Colorado. June, 1974.

Snyder, W. *Dependency in psychotherapy*. New York: Macmillan Co., 1963.

Spence, D. Lexical derivatives in patients' speech: Some new data on displacement and defense. In N. Freedman & S. Grand (Eds.). *Communicative structures and psychic structures*. New York: Plenum Press, 1977.

Spiegel, J. Some cultural aspects of transference and countertransference. In J. Masserman (Ed.). *Science and psychoanalysis* (Vol. 2). New York: Grune & Straton, 1959.

Spitz, R. Countertransference. *Journal of the American Psychoanalytic Association*, 1956, *4*,256-265.

Stern, M. (Ed.). *The other side of the couch: What therapists believe.* New York: Pilgrim Press, 1981.

Stone, L. Notes on the non-interpretative elements in the psychoanalytic situation. *Journal of the American Psychoanalytic Association*, 1956, *4*,197-223.

Sullivan, H. *The interpersonal theory of psychiatry.* New York: W. W. Norton, 1953.

Szasz, T. On the experiences of the analyst in the analytic situation. *Journal of the American Psychoanalytic Association*, 1956, *4*,197-223.

Tauber, E. Exploring the therapeutic use of countertransference. *Psychiatry*, 1954, *47*,331.

Thouless, R. The affective function of language. In M. Reyment (Ed.). *Feelings and emotions.* New York: McGraw-Hill, 1974.

Tillich, P. *Love, power and justice.* London: Oxford University Press, 1954.

Tower, L. Countertransference. *Journal of the American Psychoanalytic Association*, 1956, *4*,224-255.

Truax, C. *Toward effective counseling and psychotherapy.* Chicago: Aldine, 1967.

Tubbs, S., & Moss, S. *Human communication: An interpersonal perspective.* New York: Random House, 1974.

Uhlenheuth, E., et al. The symptomatic relief of anxiety with meprobamate, phenobarbital and placebo. *American Journal of Psychiatry*, 1959,*115*,905-910.

Veroff, J., & Veroff, J. *Social incentives.* New York: Academic Press, 1980.

————. Theoretical notes on power motivation. *Merrill-Palmer Quarterly of Behavior and Development*, 1971, *17*,59-69.

Walster, E., Walster, G., Piliavin, J., & Schmidt, L. "Playing hard to get." Understanding an elusive phenomenon. *Journal of Personality and Social Psychology*, 1973,*26*,113-121.

Weigart, E. Countertransference and self-analysis of the psychoanalyst. *International Journal of Psychoanalysis*, 1954, *35*,242.

Weisman, A. Confrontation, countertransference and context. *International Journal of Psychoanalytic Psychotherapy*, 1972, *1*(4),7-25.

Wheelis, A. *The illusionless man: Fantasies and meditations.* New York: Harper & Row, 1971.

White, B. *The origins of human competence*. Lexington, Mass.: Lexington Books, 1979.

Whitman, R., et al. Dreams about the patient: An approach to the problem of countertransference. *Journal of the American Psychoanalytic Association*, 1969, *17*,2.

Wile, D. Negative countertransference and therapist discouragement. *International Journal of Psychoanalytic Psychotherapy*, 1972, *1*(3),36-67.

Wilkins, E., & DeCharms, R. Authoritarianism and response to power cues. *Journal of Personality*, 1962, *30*,439-457.

Wilkins, W. Expectancies in applied settings. In A. Gurman & A. Razin (Eds.). *Effective psychotherapy*. Oxford: Pergamon Press, 1977.

Willis, J., & Goethals, G. Social responsibility and threat to behavioral freedom as determinants of altruistic behavior. *Journal of Personality*, 1973, *41*,376-384.

Winnicott, D. Hate in the countertransference. *International Journal of Psychoanalysis*, 1949, *30*,69.

Winter, D. *The power motive*. London: Collier MacMillan Publishing Co., 1973.

Wixen, B. *Children of the rich*. New York: Crown Publishing Co. Inc., 1973.

Wolpe, J. *The practice of behavior therapy*. New York: Pergamon Press, 1969.

Wolstein, B. *Countertransference*. New York: Grune & Stratton, 1959.

Yankelovich, D. Power and the two revolutions. In J. Masserman (Ed.). *The dynamics of power*. New York: Grune & Stratton, 1972.

Zajonc, R. Feeling and thinking: Preferences need no inferences. *American Psychologist*, 1980, *35*,151-175.

Zajonc, R., & Brickman, P. Expectancy and feedback as independent factors in task performance. *Journal of Personality and Social Psychology*, 1969, *11*,148-156.

INDEX